Praise for Revelations

"In *Revelations of the Sky*, Dr. BethAnne's words bring such warmth; she speaks of her life experiences with a profound tenderness in her heart. She allows us to personally feel what it is to be beautifully human, to sit in the uncomfortable spaces and come out stronger, to love oneself despite loss. Each passage illuminates how we have a limitless abundance of love and the capacity to live the most courageous life if we so trust in the Universe to provide such for us. Her vulnerability is woven throughout her stories and poems; she possesses an incredible gift to connect the power of words to the emotions of the heart. BethAnne's journey will inspire you to live in your heart magic, to seek out the rainbows, and to forever shine in your most radiant light."

— Dr. Alyse Snyder, Eastern Medicine
and Spiritual Retreat Leader

"Dr. BethAnne K.W's words are heavenly tuned instruments of beauty, prose and grace. In *Revelations of The Sky*, BethAnne walks us through the many colours of grief without fear, judgment or hesitation; just a knowing hand to guide the reader into the depth of their own experience by moving through hers with an open heart. From heart-achingly honest stories to breathtakingly divine poetry, *Revelations of The Sky* is a book of such sincere and spirited wisdom, I felt held amongst its pages of inimitable light. Bring your grief into a conversation with this beautiful book and let it transform your ache."

— Kris Franken, author of *The Call of Intuition*
and *Joyful Abundance Oracle Deck*

"Picking up BethAnne's book is like taking a dear friend by the hand and sitting down for a cozy, meaningful and most-heartwarming of chats, where you do most of the listening because there is so much warmth and wisdom being shared amid the sufferings of our very human lives … and you feel you are genuinely being heard at the same time. I was instantly drawn into BethAnne's world, which she so intimately and honestly relates out of what I perceive as a very earnest desire to connect with her readers and even more, for us all to commune in a shared space of healing. Her words are truly a balm. Seamlessly weaving together poetry, personal reflections and gemlike musings and affirmations, with this third book in her trilogy on grief and transition, she bravely tells of her move from Alaska to Hawaii and of the death of her beloved dog Sam. In doing so, she sends the important message that even the changes that we choose as opposed to the ones thrust upon us are not necessarily any easier to navigate, and that we should, no must, go gentle on ourselves. This is perhaps my favourite message in a book full of wholly relatable and wise words: that no matter what we have experienced, and what or whom we have lost, we can always choose to be kind to ourselves, and approach our every challenge with love. I'd like to thank BethAnne for sharing her loving and knowing heart with us so completely that she inspires us all to do the same."

— Tammy Stone Takahashi, author of the poetry collections
Formation: Along the Ganges and Back Again
(as Tammy T. Stone), and *Land*

"*Revelations of The Sky* arrived in my life at a pivotal time. I'd long been a fan of the way BethAnne creates a comforting haven with her words, a safe place to be human and experience change and grief, hope and love, right alongside her. When I read the first book of her trilogy, I relived the grief journey I'd been on (and will always be on) surrounding my mom's death. As I settled down with this third installment, I reflected on my current grief process (having lost my dad just nine months ago), and how this loss began swirling together with the anguish of losing my mom years earlier. I've been trying to process the idea of losing both beloved parents, which has effectively left me an adult orphan, plus preparing to say goodbye to our 135-year-old family homestead (built when my great-grandpa immigrated from Italy in the late 1800s).

"And I've traversed another journey similar to BethAnne's as well, an inner and outer odyssey that began in the fall of 2015, one year before my husband and I moved permanently from the U.S. to

Italy. Uprooting all that I was familiar with (culture and language and more), knowing not a soul in my new location, in a quest to get back to my roots, back to me. Taking this courageous leap into the unknown, in a country vastly different than my own, to pursue a wildly impossible dream (renovating an old villa ourselves and hosting women's retreats in our home) has been an adventure like no other. Nothing has ripped me open, and yet fulfilled me, so completely. Oh my, what an intense (and often agonizing) learning curve, a curve I admit I'm still on.

"I found solace and compassion and sisterhood in BethAnne's words. Because she knows how to write. And she knows how to write in a way that gets to the depths of your soul, taking you along on her ups and downs, visiting both triumph and despair. I needed this book right now. I'm just ending a painful two-month bout with shingles. I'm missing my sons in the states even more keenly than usual, with air travel to Europe cut off. And on the day I read the last entry, my best friend in Italy lost her mother to COVID-19. As BethAnne so beautifully notes in the passage *My Heart, My Home...* "I'm wrapping back around, spiraling deeper inside, finding a bigger sense of integration and pattern." Yes. Yes, I am. And I will probably be doing that, leaning into and learning from each physical, mental, and emotional shift, forevermore. It's nice to have company."

— April M. Lee, Holistic Life & Wellness Coach
at essence7 wellness

"This is the third in a series of books that Beth Anne began to write as she endured the power of grief losing her brother Brent. Her ability through the innocence of loss and the wisdom of her heart makes grief a powerful journey of transformation. Each word becomes an unfolding of love that provides the self-awareness and self-fulfillment we are each seeking. You will join her in her exquisite revealing of life as it embraces the beauty all around you. She writes in such a natural way that you will feel her words in the deepest part of your being, and you will know the deepest yearnings of your soul.

"This is a book you will treasure and keep by your bedside to remind you in your darkest hour that love permeates all that you are or will ever be. She will open your heart and let the light shine once again. I cannot recommend this book enough as I send people who have suffered loss to her writings and this book for me is her best."

— Janet Venturini, Spiritual Mentor & Life Coach

Revelations of The Sky

FIRST PRINT EDITION, September 2020
FIRST EBOOK EDITION, September 2020

Cover Illustration by BethAnne KW
Copyright © 2020 by BethAnne Kapansky Wright

ISBN–13: 978-1-7330099-3-5

Library of Congress Control Number: 2020945508

Printed on acid-free paper supplied by a
Forest Stewardship Council-certified provider.
First published in the United States of America
by Golden Dragonfly Press, 2020.

www.goldendragonflypress.com

www.bethannekw.com

Revelations

OF

The Sky

*133 passages on the
alchemy of grief*

Dr. BethAnne K.W.

2020
GOLDEN DRAGONFLY PRESS

To Dad and Mom.
Thank you for all your support
during this transition time.
I love you.

To Brent.
Thank you for dropping in and
helping me write this.
I love you.

To Eric.
Thank you for journeying and
growing with me through it all.
I love you.

May all beings be alive and free in love.

Contents

Sea Around Me

Earth Below Me

Fire Within Me

Sky Above Me

Opening Preview

*H*ello old friends, new friends, and grew through it with me friends.

In 2016 I first wrote *Lamentations of The Sea: 111 passages on grief, love, loss and letting go,* after losing my brother Brent. I intended for the book to be a warm friend and comfort companion to anyone in grief, and I found through the process of writing it, I came to better understand the complex nature of my grief and how my loss was changing and challenging me towards bigger growth.

Since then, *Lamentations* won a Silver Nautilus Award and was released in a 2nd edition. In the spring of 2018, I felt called to write its sequel, *Transformations of The Sun: 122 passages on finding new life after loss. Transformations* shares my spiritual journey to Kauai, my ongoing transformation through grief, and my sense of Brent's spiritual presence.

Writing the story in these books has been a highly creative and intuitive journey. I have a unique intuitive process, and in many ways, I feel the story was writing me long before I wrote the story. That is how the soul unfolds: it writes us and sings us and moves us into being when we say *yes* to its call.

Revelations of The Sky: 133 passages on the alchemy of grief is the last collection of my experiences completing the *Lamentations* trilogy. Like the first two books, told through poetry, prose, essays and personal reflections, *Revelations* explores the strange alchemy of grief, the phenomenal power of love, and diving into the journey of being both fully human and divine.

It is a work that is personal, psychological, creative and spiritual. Though the passages in these books are heavily layered with what I understand to be messages of spirit from multiple channels, I find that the deeper I go on my spiritual journey, the less inclined I am to try and qualify, define, or shape matters of the mystic realm. I'd rather allow them to qualify, define, and shape me, so I can keep becoming my highest expression of self.

The words in this book are my experiences. I've put them into language the best I know how, and I will leave it up to you, wonderful reader, to take what you will from them in the hopes they bring light to your path and encouragement to keep working out your unique and beautiful relationship with the mysteries.

Mostly I hope the words encourage you to explore the possibility of you, to find the love in grief, to bravely allow for your highest expression, and to keep working on your unique and beautiful relationship with your heart for that is where our truest wealth always lays.

In hope,
Dr. BethAnne K.W.

Prologue: The Invitation

Dive into
the universe's
space.

Let it take you
on a wild ride
filled with
moonlight
and grace.

Slipstream
& stardream in
akasha's bright
face —

Riding the rhymes
of the cosmos
light rays.

Rippling
tripling
trickling
waves.

Magic is found
in the everyday,
when we get out
of our own way —

And learn how
to lean into
Love.

Sea Around Me

Everybody
finds their
light and shines
at their own
pace in their
own time.

1

Rainbow Bridge

*L*ittle Sister, if I could take it from you, your sadness, I would. There's no sadness where I'm at — only love and understanding. I remember feeling sad in my life on earth, but I can't tell you why, now it feels so far away.

I can't take the sadness away from you Little Sister, because you're in a different place.

But I can tell you, as much as you can, to find the jubilation and joy. That is what I would want for you: for you to know I am happy and to find happiness too.

It's not an easy road you walk, Little Sister. There is help along the way, so you don't have to walk it alone. *Know you are never alone, and it will make things lighter.*

Thor's rainbow bridge wasn't that far off. There's much that lays beyond what you can see. But I know you see it anyway. You learned how to see me when I was no longer there except in spirit. You see the other worlds that can't be seen with the eyes.

Someday Little Sister, when you're ready, I will tell you more about them. But for now, be where you're at. There's a reason for it. We learn that here — that it's all working together.

You've shown such faith Little Sister, don't stop now. Remember: *Goonies never say die and they never give up.*

2

REVOLVING DOORS

*C*hange is the way of life. I try and stay open to change and let myself unform, flow, and let go, though it's not always easy. Sometimes resistance creeps in at unexpected times in unexpected ways.

Our upstairs neighbors moved yesterday — we rent the downstairs of a giant home, up in the hills of Kauai, and they rented the upstairs. Though we had a few intersections in the almost year we've been here, we weren't close and sometimes I found their noise disruptive. So, I found myself surprised by a sense of sadness and loss I didn't understand or expect when we watched them drive off last night.

On to a new life in a new state for a new job.

As I reflected on my feelings about the situation, I realized they were our first neighbors on the island, and I am used to their presence, routines, and sounds. There was a sense of pattern and familiarity to things. *Sometimes there is a sense of loss when something familiar changes.* New neighbors mean new and unknown presence, routines, and sounds, and the unknown can be hard.

Also, I realize the awareness they were leaving, coupled with watching the movers come and go — all while empathically sensing the neighbor's stress, sadness, and excitement — time warped me back to a year ago in Alaska when we were getting ready to move to Kauai.

All those feelings of leave-takings, goodbyes, and the surrealism of ending life in Anchorage rose up, leaving me with a soft sense of nostalgia and a wistful longing. A longing which reminded me when we were leaving Alaska, I was in the middle of so much change. I believed moving here would create a new foundation and sense of stability.

Instead, I have found the new foundation is still being created and more change has come my way. It's been a long time since I've had a sense of certitude in my life. I have an ongoing question of who I'll be and what I'll be doing, as I continue going through personal metamorphosis.

Sometimes I wonder, if I wandered back into my old spaces in Anchorage, if I would hold the new shape I've taken here. Or would I find myself shifting to still try and fit those old spaces? I have a feeling it would be difficult to maintain my shape.

All spaces have energetic imprints and patterns. The longer we are in them, the stronger and deeper those patterns pull. It can be hard to form anew when we continue to occupy the same space.

Sometimes I have to remind myself I am living exactly what I signed up for: change, life transition, a new creative process, a deeper more beautiful relationship with the universe, and a deeper relationship of trust with spirit.

I chose my lack of certitude. Life was too well formed and well grooved in Anchorage, and I needed to be an unmolded lump of clay, so I could create something new. That doesn't mean my choice hasn't left me highly uncomfortable at times, forcing me to find stability and comfort in the middle of shifting sands.

The ocean helps with that. As does hiking my favorite mountain. Our fur kids. Writing. Listening to the jungle green. Making art out of confusion. Embracing the spirit of creativity. Grounding into love, and earth, and Mother Kauai.

I feel a part of this island now. She gives me permission to release my old Alaskan identity and honor that former shell of self. But here is where I belong, and where I need to be for who I'm growing into. This island has a way of moving life along and bringing healing about. Sometimes in places we didn't realize we needed.

Small island. Big impact. Wild change.

As such, even though I hoped for a weekend of quiet regrouping in an empty house after the chaos of the departing neighbors, I shouldn't have been surprised when our old neighbors drove off and into a new future within an hour, we had new ones moving in.

I met the husband. He seems nice. We talked about cats, and he apologized for the noise. The conversation left me hopeful and optimistic.

Even though somebody else lived here just yesterday, and the turnaround time is like a revolving door — it isn't yesterday. It's today. *A new day with new people and new ways, and at times change quickly revolves and evolves us.*

Change is life's way. It certainly is this island's way. It can be sad and hard, but all we can do is embrace the flow and honor whatever feelings come up in our own waters. Knowing the universe works in ebbs and flows and feelings — *like seasons, like life, and like us* — are all fluid and will always shift.

We just have to trust when we lean into the flow, we will be taken in whatever direction we most need to go.

3

Unleash

My dear one,
don't you know
when an old
cycle ends,
a new one
begins,
and anything
you think you'll lose
will come around
in new form?

Transience
is life's variance,
the grace of change
soul's interface,
and my dear one,
I know it's hard,
but we grow
more through
letting go
than we do
when we
hang on.

So, remember
any release
is also relief,
allowing the
energy of
what we unleash
to find its wings,
return to love,
and be
renewed
reformed
redeemed.

4

Strings

*H*ow human it is to want to hold onto something. Yet how transcendent it is to let go in love. An act which speaks to the core of unconditional love.

Because unconditional love releases strings and expectations. It just is. Pure and undiluted in any situation. We learn to love simply for the act of loving, without an expectation attached to what and who we love.

We learn to love without promises or guarantees. And so, if a time comes when that which we love needs to change or grow, we can choose to unstring, release, and let go.

5

The Field

Every field and flower fades, but love is infinite.
— MELANIE CHISHOLM

*W*e found out today our senior dog, Sam, has cancer. A beautiful morning at the beach, where he laid by the ocean and sunned himself, turned into a nightmare of a seizure just an hour later on the car ride home, turned into rushing to the vet, turned into cancer.

It's a rough blow.

I am grateful for the sequence of events though, which helped us get him immediate medical attention. It was not a coincidence we happened to be a few minutes away from the vet's office. Nor was it happenstance the head vet was there to tend to him, and the usually busy clinic was almost empty.

He had a lot of care, and the timing reminded me: *I am not alone in this.*

He's sleeping peacefully at my feet now, and we are left with uncertainty and hard decisions.

I knew when I adopted an older dog, he would cross the rainbow bridge sooner rather than later. He was guesstimated to be 8–10 when we got him in 2014, which puts him around 12–14 now. I'd hoped he'd be one of those unstoppable older dogs who makes it to 16–18.

It is difficult to love brave in this world.

Anybody who says love is just about the light is skipping over the part where being human can be hard. It is in this space we learn love is also about the grit. *It's messy. It breaks our hearts. Sometimes it's lotus love, which swirls us around and sinks us deeper into the mud before our petals are formed.* Sometimes love just straight up hurts and aches.

I know some people would rather wall themselves off to the pain. I understand that, it feels terrible to hurt this way. I've cried all afternoon and know there are more tears to come. Yet living numb isn't living.

Open-hearted living is the only form of living that makes sense to me because it's the only way I can feel all the beauty, joy, and light that exists in this world too, even if it means I have to crawl through the mud sometimes. The only thing I know to help find solace during those times of ache is the knowledge: *every time life has cracked my heart wide open it grows in love, and I always come through the dark passage with a new diamond of light.*

Always.

I learned that lesson after a painful divorce, which was the catalyst for my spiritual awakening. I learned it triple-fold when my sweet dog Pepe passed away in 2013, and I chose to love him through it with beauty and bravery. I cemented that lesson when my brother crossed over in 2016. Despite all the horrible grief and terrible pain, he left me with so many gifts of light, I was able to take my grief and transform it into gold, transforming myself in the process.

I can only assume that when Sam's time comes, he'll have his own gold and diamonds of light to gift me. Diamonds and diamonds and diamonds. He already has just by blessing me with his presence in my life.

For today though, I'm a grief-filled fur momma who is committed to doing right by our sweet kid, listening to what he has to tell us about his health, and trusting for wisdom and clarity to guide us to the right decisions.

I'm hoping we have more time.

More trips to the beach, more car rides, more sweet moments where he blesses me with the energy of unconditional love he embodies so beautifully (though I'm wise enough to know that when it's time to let go I will let go, as that too is part of love).

Earlier this week, I took him and his younger brother Frodo up to Kokee State Park. We drove up, up, up on the twisty, turny, windy road. Through red dirt, Hawaiian pines, cooler temperatures and canyon vistas. We stopped at the lodge. There are trails at the park with much better views, but they're too hard for Sam's old body to traverse, so I would have had to leave Sam behind, and no way was I leaving Sam behind.

He is too much of my heart.

The lodge is perfect for our needs. Outside, a huge grassy picnic area resides, surrounded by remarkable old trees whose faces look so calm and wise you know they've witnessed the passage of time. Their sage, grounded energy reminds me — *for every cycle that ends a new one begins, every death a rebirth, and all things eventually come back round again.*

Sam lays in the middle of the field, stretching out in the sunshine, happy with warmth and fresh air. Frodo and I circle the field, exploring knobby trunks, making friends with the ancient grove, as I contemplate how I'd rather be wandering the field with my curious pup, smiling at the pleasure radiating off of contented old Sam, than doing anything else.

Soaking up the love, cherishing the honor of getting to be the human for these two precious beings for whatever time I'm given with each of them. Saying thank you to the earth and the sky and the trees and all that IS — over and over and over again — for the gift that is this life.

6

CYCLES

I always say that Love wears a million faces. But so do other things. Grief and Sorrow. Compassion and Kindness. Beauty. Holiness. Grace. Faith. Hope. Love is just the tie that binds and wraps around it all.

We can think we have an emotional territory navigated and figured out, and it can shock and surprise us when we find ourselves tripping and floundering. Or feeling lost and disoriented in a space we thought we knew.

The thing about our Life Journey is we don't pass through the same territory twice.

Just because we thought we knew sorrow, because of a previous experience, doesn't mean sorrow will feel the same with what's happening now. Just because we thought we knew grief because we've already undertaken a grief passage, doesn't mean grief won't knock us sideways and teach us new gifts when it shows back up in our lives.

Just because we thought we knew what love was doesn't mean Love won't have new ways of sneaking up, surprising us and teaching us more of its faces. Teaching us new psalms, lamentations, transformations, and revelations. Teaching us how love truly is the core underlying all, so it can always be found anywhere. No matter the emotional territory.

Emotions are fluid, so are our life experiences, and so are we. Which means we continually have learning opportunities and mastery opportunities. Just like the moon, and the sun, and the seasons — we too go through multiple cycles throughout our lives.

It is how we grow, how we deepen, how we evolve, and how our hearts get bigger. As we travel closer to the truth of our souls in a constant dance of ebb and flow.

7

PEARL

*T*hey say the best way to learn something is to teach it.

I teach grief. I already know the language fairly well, I learned to speak it fluently when going through the loss of my brother, and in that fluency, I took my words, wrote a book, and have been an author and voice on grief since.

It's not that I think I've learned grief's lessons — *I will forever be learning and relearning some of those lessons.* But since Brent passed in 2016, the heart of my grief is further away than what it once was. Those ripping rage reds and stormy navy blues in my alchemy have quieted to softer pinks and deeper grays, with only occasional bursts of loud color.

The grief is still there, but it's different.

Then last week, when we got the news of Sam's cancer and were told he has about 6 months, maybe less, I realized I have new reds and blues and eruptions of color exploding all over my heart palette.

There have been moments this week where I've felt like my heart is going to rip itself out of my chest, it feels so heavy and hurt. It's suffering break and ache, and I'm trying to attend to it as best as I can. Sam is still with us, but there is an anticipatory loss from the concrete knowledge we're going into all the lasts. Last summer. Last memories. Last moments.

I keep looking at him — he holds so much of my heart — and cannot imagine life without him, even as I know I'll be okay, because I have enough love inside of me to get through this.

The profundity of my grief, as I write these words, is such that my eyes are so raw I've taken to wearing sunglasses in public, my throat is full of the unshed, and I've found myself doing tasks of grief that surprised even me.

I spontaneously had the compulsion to buy a special bear necklace to wear during this time period, so I could associate it with Sam, my "Baby Bear," and have something tangible to link to the memories created this last summer.

I started to make a list of all my memories and musings of Sam, doing my best to fill in the timeline since he came into our hearts in November 2014. Some of my happiest memories are on that list, and I'm touched and awestruck at the magnitude of love wrapped up in his being.

It's like I'm trying to piece our timeline together and take stock of who he's been to me, how this special being has changed my life, and what pieces of my heart he holds.

I put together an album of all the pictures I have of Sam. Not only to have something tangible to look at, but as a way to track the evolution of time and to acknowledge all the life passages he's seen me through and all the memories we've created.

And I reread some of the passages in my grief book from fresh eyes:

"There is no shame to be found in having a hurting heart when your hopes haven't gone as planned and life has brought you to a point of break. No shame at all. Your heart is doing what it is built to do: love, feel, break, heal.

The human heart is one of the most achingly fragile and sturdily resilient forces on the planet. Don't be afraid of what it has to say. Don't be afraid of its depths. And don't be afraid to let it do what it needs to do to release, remember, repair, renew."

I found my 2018 self, learning from my 2016 self. I almost felt like I was reading somebody else's words as I sat there nodding, "yes, yes, this is exactly how I feel, somebody understands."

Dogs often reflect back a piece of our own soul we aren't able to put words to.

They love unconditionally and there is an absence of judgment that allows a purity of love. They see our soul-light and what is best in us. They offer love without expectation. *Dogs love us regardless of who we are or what we do.*

It struck me earlier this week I need to work on loving Sam like this now. I had hoped and expected we would have him longer, but he doesn't owe me my expectations. Neither does life.

So, now it's my job to love him without expectation of timeline. Without expectation of what will come to pass. Without expectation — just purity of intent.

I know more burning tears and heart swells and chest aches are coming, and that's okay, *that's part of love.* I find it so beautiful I've had the privilege to love so deeply it hurts this badly, because all the hurt is there because of all the love.

The hurt is the grain of sand — the irritant in the oyster — but the love is the protective layer I will keep covering the grain with over and over. I figure the best I can do is to follow my own advice: *love, feel, break, heal, release, remember, repair, renew,* and keep finding the love to cover the grain until it becomes a magnificent pearl.

8

BEAUTY WAY

If a lone
flower
can find
the beauty
needed to bloom
in the midst
of ugliness —
so can you.

9

THE TEACHER

A Dog's life will witness many things.
Turning of seasons, changing of self. Moves and relocations. Graduations and celebrations and lamentations. They will find the love in all of it and simply meet us where we are at.

A dog's life will bear testament to many things.

Silent watchers, they are timekeepers who keep track of our days with pats, wags, walks, treats, and quiet pools of eyes who see the best in us. The bond is one which often defies words, because animals communicate differently.

They speak without words. Through body language, and facial expressions, and their own special noises, and silent signals. They speak with the energetic frequency of love, which is a resonance that reflects back to us our better selves.

Dogs usually come into our lives already resonating love fluently, but it's a heart language human-beings spend their lifetime learning.

A dog's life will teach us many things.

They have their priorities straight and well-organized hearts, which translates in their silent wisdom. Observers, passengers, joy bringers, heart-fillers: they teach us and when our teacher is physically gone, there's so much emptiness, but also so much love.

That is the journey of a dog.

They come here knowing what we have forgotten: the purpose of a soul is to simply show up and bring in the grace of unconditional love. Dogs already know that, so they don't need to travel here as long as we. They leave us the gift of memory, and more importantly the lasting effects of what their presence awakens in us:

A heart can become closer to Love, because of the love of a Dog.

10

Ramble on Rose

We can't go back again; we can only return to the love inside.

I t is the perfect day. One of my favorite memories. Labor Day weekend, 2016. McCarthy. A long, bumpy road to endless wilderness, leading to a hidden town accessed by foot over a bridge, with a cold winding river under, and a cluster of rust-red old mine buildings high on a hill.

Kennicott. The last weekend the lodge is open before shutting down for the season until the next summer. There is an air of excitement, bittersweet, and the kind of wistful nostalgia that hits on the last day of summer camp among everyone we talk to.

"Just like crazy Otto, just like wolfman jack, sittin' plush with a royal flush, aces back to back. Just like Mary Shelly, just like Frankenstein, clank your chains and count your change and try to walk the line."

We camp that crisp September night in the back of my truck, "Beastie," we appointed her. Once my brother's, now mine, her all-terrain wheels gifting us with adventuring into back country all summer long, as we created our summer of "lasts" in Alaska.

This particular weekend, we explore the area by running on a sunny bluebird Alaska day, which brings an extra layer of magic to the old mine buildings, yellowing trees, bountiful glaciers, and rugged setting.

"I'm gonna sing you a hundred verses in ragtime, I know this song it ain't never gonna end. I'm gonna march you up and down along the county line, Take you to the leader of a band."

Sam and Frodo are with us. Sam waits faithfully in the car while the three of us go on our exploratory run, we rush back wanting to make sure he doesn't get too hot in the sun. The rest of the afternoon is spent by the churning river, napping in the bed of my Durango, listening to the Grateful Dead sing "Ramble on Rose."

It is golden. Everything converges that day into an unplanned moment of perfection. Beautiful setting. A sense of overwhelming love and belonging with my family. Napping in the sun listening to Jerry Garcia sing on. In that moment of love and light, I feel infinite, limitless, part of the oneness.

"Did you say your name was ramblin' rose? Ramble on baby, settle down easy. Ramble on rose."

It is a weekend that represents the best of our family. The best of Alaska. Brent's loss is 8 months ago — enough distance to finally feel goodness again. Kauai is still 10 months away — far enough where it is still a silver-edged, hopeful dream.

The blue skies and warm sunshine glint off the already golden leaves of fall, and it makes me want to believe we can push the sun back up in the sky and live in the seam of possibility — suspended between two seasons, resting in the lull where everything is ripe and possible.

"Good-bye mama and papa. Good-bye Jack and Jill. The grass ain't greener. The wine ain't sweeter. Either side of the hill."

The treetops look significantly different from where I now sit. I know, with pangs of longing and loss, I will never go back to McCarthy, I don't live in Alaska anymore. I won't sit by the churning river, reminisce on the past, and remember our first time there in honor and memory of Sam.

We don't have as many memories on Kauai with Sam as we did in Alaska, and there's grief tied into that. And there are days where I just want to crawl back into my memory, return to that golden space of certainty and live in the warm reflection of what was, even as my heart hurts, thrusts, grieves and tries to remember:

We can't go back again; we can only return to the love inside.

11

Finding Home

When did
last summer become
a fading memory,
and when did this summer
become the days
whose breaths
I beat and
breathe?

I traded the blush
of the lavender trees
and pink peonies
and soft fireweed
for the jungle green,
and the scent of the sea
and the hints of tuberose,
which waft with
evening's warm
breeze.

I traded the feel
of summer's endless peaks,
autumn's golden leaves,
winter's silver freeze
for ocean's blue ease
and sunshine dreams,
and an island of magic
and mystery.

I traded the grace
of goose lake's geese
and light's solstice sweep
and bird ridge's steep
for the ooze of heat
and a softer me

and a chance
to be bigger,
to be more,
to be free.

Yet maybe there
will always be
a part of me
beating in the earth
I've left behind,
in the rosy tundra
and shale gray mountains
and the evergreens
of arctic pines.

Even as I learn to
embrace these days
create new ways
and ride the waves,
of change that ring
with heart's goodbye —

*Finding my home
in the seam of these times.*

12

My Heart, My Home

*M*y mentor says I do my emotional work fast, and this is true. I'm well-practiced at it, and the language of emotions and the heart is the language I speak best. This week is no exception — with the news of Sam's cancer, I've found myself swimming in feeling's deep.

Swimming. Diving. Treading. Exploring. Going under. Kicking hard to break the surface and move towards the light.

Processing Sam has me processing myself, and I'm finding I'm wrapping back around, spiraling deeper inside, finding a bigger sense of integration and pattern.

When I first arrived on Kauai last July, I needed space from Alaska. I had just been through a vast amount of tumult to manifest the move. Arriving on the island brought me the same sensation I always have after a marathon when I finally cross the finish line: fatigued, relieved, gratified, tired, reflecting on all it took to get to the finish.

Looking forward to a good shower, clean clothes, and a huge meal. Looking forward to taking a break from training for a while. I've always been the kind of runner who trains in ebbs and flows, and I enjoy my off season when I don't have to worry about logging miles.

When I first got to the island, I didn't have to worry about logging miles.

It wasn't a time for deep process work or heavy emotional labor. It was a time of light, summer, rainbows, and slipping into my mermaid skin, so I could be present in the new place and my new home.

Now it's almost a year later, and I find myself revisiting the concept of home. They say home is where the heart is, and I have always found this to be true, yet there are multidimensional layers which constitute home — *house, location, family, belonging, connection, love.* There are many ways we define home.

Sam's cancer has been a catalyst to work through my relationship with home. The complexity of my grief is heart-achingly substantial, but as I've deciphered its stratum, I've come to understand the breadth of my attachment in deeper ways.

Sam's presence in my life has seen me through significant passages including buying a home, getting married, losing my brother, quantum leaps of personal transformation, selling a home, closing a practice, leaving Alaska, moving to Kauai, and reestablishing a new life here, which is still a process undergoing construction.

That's an awful lot of change for a 10-pound dog, who looks like a walking stuffed animal, to witness. Yet, he's witnessed all and just accepted and loved us wherever we are at.

Samwise is a fundamental part of my concept of home and has been since he entered our lives. We had a joyful young pup and the mercurial presence of a cat, but I knew our home needed the love of an old dog.

When Sam showed up in November of 2014, it was seamless. The adoption center brought him over, and he settled down on the couch like he already lived there. Even pup and cat accepted him, and within days we wondered how we ever got by without our Sam.

I found myself cycling back to 2014 this past weekend.

We had a terrific house in Alaska. I loved our space and called it the Rainbow Cottage in The Woods. If there was ever an external space that matched my internal space it was that house. Colorful, filled with love and life, hidden trinkets and jewels in all sorts of nooks and crannies.

Right by the trail system. Rainbow walls, potted plants, vintage furniture, and whimsical art curated an eclectic, cheerful feel. It perfectly supported our family's needs down to the cozy back patio, which caught the sunset and lingering light, and the front porch, which caught the morning sunrise and day's warmth.

That porch was my sanctuary the summer after my brother died.

The winter had been cold, gray, gritty, and dark. It echoed the annihilation and wasteland I felt inside.

Summer came early that year. The lilac bushes opened at May's beginning; the grass soon emerald. I filled the porch with basket upon basket of bright flowers creating an oasis I thought of as my secret garden. Flame fuchsia, hot orange, happy yellow, vibrant purple, deep red, electric violet: my grieving heart craved color and life, and I drank up the blooms, summer breezes, and gentle skies in great gulps.

I was content to sit, read, write, and be on the porch as much as I could. It was medicine for my broken being; wildflowers for my soul, which planted themselves in my grief space, reminding me life and beauty still go on.

I still have a visceral felt sense of that time, those blooms, and that version of self who was covered by the grace of Summer 2016. I miss that house and all it represented.

It was hard to leave it behind, and yet I knew we couldn't stay in Alaska just because of a home — not when my soul was insistently calling me to Kauai. My brother helped me let go. I kept reminding myself: *if you can let go of Brent, you can let go of your stuff.*

I trusted something better was waiting in Kauai.

I left behind the lilac bushes and arctic roses for plumeria trees and cherry hibiscus. Those crisp, sunny Alaskan summer days have given way to the humid, balmy tropics. Hours in the mountains have now become hours by the sea. Mountain shale is now red dirt trail. Favorite haunts and favorite places are being discovered and redefined.

The memories I have here aren't as thick and deep, but sometimes we have to make new memories and create new meaning.

I needed to become something different and something *other* over here, and it's important I remind myself of that.

As I've time traveled, warp zoned, and spiraled back to my Alaskan life, I've visited many remembrances in mind, heart and in photos; smiling with tenderness, poignancy, gratitude, and a bit of longing.

I'll admit it's hard to be unformed and living in a rented space, even though we've done our best to make it feel like home. I've wondered since I came to the island where and what our future home will be. While the place we've initially landed is a good space to get us going and see us through this first year, it's not Home with a capital H. It's just home for now.

There is a part of me who yearns for the familiar and known of home. Last weekend I sorted through old pictures and imagined what it would be like to drive down Turnagain Arm again. Climb Indian House Peak. Stop at the grocery on the way back for tasty treats and snacks, then settle into our bright green den for a movie night while all three pets cuddle close.

As I've sat with my yearnings, I am able to acknowledge as wonderful as that space was, there was nothing new for me to learn there. If I had stayed, there would have been more summers on the porch and winters in the mountains. More rainbow home, cozy moments, and happy memories.

But there would not be growth. Alaska had become a beautiful incubator by the end.

I felt so boxed in within the bounds of my old life, and I know the claustrophobic feeling I had begun to associate with Alaska would have become increasingly intolerable. Sam would still be sick, and we'd be facing his inevitable loss. I would still be feeling confined, constricted, and over-burdened by carrying my practice while trying to free something inside of me, which didn't have creative, spiritual, or energetic space to grow.

I wouldn't have experienced the growth and change I've experienced this past year had I not thrown myself into the great unknown.

Alaska was the known. Kauai has been nothing but change and unknowing.

Alaska was certitude and stability. Kauai is creative evolution and flow.

Alaska relied on my own devices, familiar grooves and ruts, and the security of my practice. Kauai relies on spirit, trust, and intuition that I'm following my calling and becoming my True Self.

Alaska was easy. Kauai is a wild ride: It's a different kind of summer and a different kind of home. But it *is* home now, and I can't go back. Even if I could, it would never be the same. That is the grace of the transience of life.

Sam reminds me of this daily, as I can see he's at peace with his journey, and he seems to know his time to go will be soon, and he only wants to be close to his beings these last months. I can also see he has loved every moment he's been a part of our family and will continue to love and accept us, just as we are, until he knows it's time to let go.

I'm doing my best to simply love him and to pour him, our memories, and the love we have cherished into my heart, so I'll take it with me always. Because this I do know — houses may change, locations may change, relationships may change, moments may change, life may change, but the love inside will never change, and it is the surest compass I've found to always bring myself back to a space of home.

Which brings me back to the concept: *home is where the heart is.*

I can't return to my old space in Alaska, which represented a brief, perfect moment in time. I can hold its lessons in my heart though. I can pour into me the memory of watching the winter solstice sky shift from blue to lavender to pink to black, as I sit on my red couch with the cheerful yellow walls, while lights from the Christmas tree sparkle and the fur kids gather.

I can tuck in the memories of taking bubble baths in our mustard yellow tub — I was undeterred by the color and simply painted the bathroom turquoise and put up mermaid and beach art — while Sam lays on a nearby rug. *Merpup we call him for his love of being by the water.*

I can remember summers on the porch, surrounded by colorful flowers. First came the blooming of the lilac bush. Then the pink peonies. Then the marshy mushrooms, which marked the passage of summer into fall, as the midnight sun gradually began to set earlier, and a softer hush came to the air when the leaves turned from September's gold into October's cranberry dusk.

I can pour into me all that was best. All that was love. All that was beautiful about those times.

You can't take it with you, but you do take your heart with you, and so anything we've integrated into our heart continues to nourish and nurture us. *Just like Sam.* This summer I'll be pouring him into my heart. Pouring in the memories. Pouring in the love. Pouring in the best parts of the word home.

It's raining outside as I write these words. Sam is lying next to me. The jungle is misty, and I'm tucked into my office. I did take a few precious items from my old home in Alaska to recreate a rainbow cottage feel in this space, and it soothes me and brings a sense of continuity to a year that has been a rocky bridge year, as we work on establishing our new home.

I am so grateful Sam is still here with us and will always be part of those first memories we created in Kauai. I keep reminding myself to try to find the love, wherever I'm planted, and everything will be all right.

I called my mentor the other day to process my loss. She knew Samwise well, he always came to appointments with me, and she remembered fondly the sweet, gentle presence he brought to her office.

"Sam had the capacity to attach deeply and purely. He had the ability to walk into any space, accept it exactly where it was at, and simply bring it love. Just like you BethAnne. Don't you see? Sam and you reflect that in one another. You are kindred spirits."

It might be the best thing anyone has ever said to me.

13

COLLECTOR OF HOPE

I am a collector
of hope.

Life shows me
loss, and I'll
show Life *Love*,
because pearls
are formed
when we
heap
the good
upon the rub
of hard grain.

I am a collector
of hope.

You tell me I can't,
and I will tell you
about possibility
and dream
and perseverance.

I am a collector
of hope.

Show me the worst,
and I'll find the best.
Show me the hurting,
and I'll find the beauty.
Show me your soul,
and I'll see your light.
Show me the dark,
and I'll remind you
that is the space

where the
stars gleam
and guide.

I am a collector
of hope.

It's who I am.
It's what I do.
It's all I be.

Grabbing it into me
in fistfuls
and armfuls
and bountiful grasps —

Like raindrops in
a bucket of love,
I look for ways to
garner hope.

14

THAT'S HOPE

*I*t is difficult to find a sense of hope that transcends circumstances. This world can be a cruel and callous place, and it's easy to fall into despair and hopelessness. Yet there is more good than bad, more beauty than ugly, more light than dark — we just don't always see the hope that's there.

But it is there.

Every time a cruelty happens, and you let your heart feel and break and reform — you create an energetic act of reparation, mending, and restoration in the spaces where hearts are closed in this world. And that's hope.

Every time you ask yourself, "what can I possibly do," and you do something through the act of writing, speaking, praying, calling, thinking, creating, awakening, talking, sharing, singing, transforming, and any other act that keeps you open and caring instead of numb? That's hope.

Every time you try and right a wrong. Regardless of what happens. Your effort is seen and valued by unseen eyes and carries a ripple effect of goodness. And that's hope.

Every time your efforts feel like they don't matter, or didn't make a difference, or didn't have the consequence you expected, yet you choose to return to a space of love? That's hope.

Every time you choose compassion over hate. Every time you refine your rage over injustice into informed action. Every time you sink your heels into the gritty mud of love, and you refuse to accept despair as your set point? That's hope.

It's easy to maintain hope when things go right, but it is hard, hard, hard when they don't. When you hurt. When something breaks. When you see intentional apathy. When your stomach plummets sick and your heart cracks wide over calculated cruelty.

It's easy to get lost in all that's wrong, but there is more love in this world than not. I don't believe this world would still be going if it wasn't so: hate destroys absolutely, and love heals absolutely. We are still here, which means Love is stronger.

So, if you are struggling with hopelessness, remember you're not alone. There is a whole world of people taking a stand for something better. Speaking up and speaking out when they feel something is wrong. Praying in quiet hours. Doing things behind the scenes which receive no recognition, yet whose impact carries far. Sending mindful intentions of love out into the ether, so good intentions sprinkle down and land where light is most needed.

There is an entire world of people who are being Love's hands and heart by reaching up, and out, and down, and over, and across, and far as they bring love into the spaces they touch.

And that's hope.

Because every one of these beings, in their own unique way and soul path, is holding space on this planet for more love, more peace, more grace, and more compassion. Being a space holder is not something to take lightly. It is tough, messy, work that requires us to keep getting up every time we get knocked down by those who are not about holding space for light.

But you are holding space. I am holding space. We are holding space.

There's so many of us, from all different walks and beliefs, and we are in this together — holding space, being harbingers of light, refusing to settle for less than love.

And that's hope.

That's hope.

15

Canon in Trust

I 've come to see through my journeys into grief that self-trust is a vital element for the process of the griever.

Self-trust becomes necessary in grief, so we can give ourselves permission to be exactly where we are at. To feel what we feel. To love as we love. To grieve as we see fit. To heal, mend, break and reknit. To stay open to our process of self, which is absolutely valid and deserves our attention, care, and trust.

Our experience of self is the experience, which informs us the most, therefore we have to learn to trust it. We have to trust our flashes of intuition and sparks of knowing. Our heart-songs and belly-flutters and soul-canons, which work together to chart our course and guide us along our path.

We have to trust the broken spaces where we grieve and the smile lines where we joy. Trust our perceptual sensitivities and unique frameworks for looking at life. Trust in the ways we feel called to love, and how we feel called to love.

We can remain open-minded and teachable, while still fundamentally returning to an informed core space, where we sit with our inner wisdom and examine what holds right and true for us.

Because we are the only ones who will embody our space of self.

We are the only ones who can learn to find peace inside of ourselves and honor our experience of living in a way that satisfies our personal requirements of soul. We are the only ones who can listen to our heart-lights, navigate our change-points, and be our own truth-guides.

For that we need trust. Big trust. Self trust. Heart trust. Soul trust.

Each of us exploring ourselves. Learning about ourselves. Doing the work of self to find growth where we need, roots where we sink, and mending where we bleed. A loving of self, so deep, the obfuscation of this world can give way to a clearer heart-seeing.

16

BRUISES

$\mathcal{S}$ ome days are so tender, we feel bruised by the very act of waking up. Grief hits, trauma rears, sadness or badness or grayness sneaks in blinking rapidly — sometimes humaning is hard.

Vulnerability has the capacity to sink us or swim us; often it does both and after dropping into ocean's darker depths, we find enough of a push to move towards the light and break through.

Remember those hard days are not a measure of anything other than being real and being here and grappling with the full scope of self. They are part of being human, part of living in a hardened world, and part of undoing the hardness and exposing our layers piece by piece, as we get closer to our softness and deepest heart truth.

Sometimes we bruise in the process.

Take a cue from water on those days and just be. No more or no less than your most broken piece. Feelings are mutable and require room to breathe. Healing comes when we allow our whole selves the space to release and be free.

17

*T*HICK AND *T*HIN

I t is difficult to trust in uncertain times.

Trust Life. Trust the Process. Trust Spirit. Trust Higher Power. Trust Ourselves. Trust it will all work out.

There are many dimensions and layers of trust, and yet it all melts down to the same core truth — *either we trust things are moving towards our highest good, or we don't.*

At least that's how it translates in my mind as I come back round to the question of, "BethAnne, do you believe the universe supports you or not?" Because my answer to that question makes all the difference in my mental and emotional state and how I navigate my life.

I write these words as Sam lays near me, laboring to breathe. His cancer seems to be worsening. All the plans I had for today have been deferred to just be present with him, watch over him, and be available for care.

This news has come during a rocky season in life. Not rocky-awful per se, but not rocky-road ice-cream-awesome either. Just rocky in the sense I've been in a change cycle since moving to Kauai. Almost everything has been in flux.

So many questions still unanswered. I'm still waiting for pieces to come together as I look to my own future and try and piecemeal a new path as a writer, healer, artist, teacher, and per-haps something else I don't quite have words or vision for yet.

Also, since we've been on the island, my husband's initial job loss and subsequent job search were hard on him and incredibly tough. Currently, the resulting job is hard on him and incredibly tough. So, he's trying to piece himself and find his way too.

Somewhere in the middle of that, the news of Sam's cancer emerged, and our family is working through anticipatory loss and grief. We call Sam the glue of our family, because he has a way of bringing us together. *Now, we're left wondering what we'll do without our Sam and what might fall apart when he goes.*

The wiser part of me knows everything has a time and a season. Especially old dogs.

It is difficult to trust in uncertain times.

These are the times that pull at what is most human in us and what is most vulnerable. These are the times where difficult feeling states get triggered. Emotions like discouragement, sadness, doubt, fear, and anxiety come parading into our inner domains, creating a mess in their wake.

It takes a lot of grounding not to let them run the show.

It takes a lot of emotional courage to examine what those parts of our self have to say, where those feelings are coming from, and to acknowledge and make space for them.

It takes A LOT of trust to breathe deep and find what we need to override their cacophony, finding our heart center and stillness in the swirl.

It is difficult to trust in uncertain times.

Life happens to us all — experiences that run the gambit from beautiful to horrible, and it just seems to be part and parcel of the whole deal of being human.

I try and remember things aren't always what they seem: beautiful things can come from awful things, and things that seemed beautiful sometimes don't work out so well. *We learn, and grow, and experience, and reach, and stretch, and grow some more as we go through it all.*

Trusting can be hard, and I offer no easy solution. Each of us is navigating our relationship with life and that's something we can only work out on our own. But for myself, I keep coming back to this sticking point — *either I believe Life is on my side or I don't.*

If I believe Life is on my side, then I do not need to fear and worry. At this point in my life, hard though it may sometimes be, I do believe this truth, because I've experienced its veracity many times.

I believe Life is on my side.

And I have a dear old dog, who's breathing finally relaxed, sleeping by my side. Trusting me with his love and care for the last part of his journey. He's right to trust — his trust is not misplaced — there is no way I would ever let him down.

My love for him is too absolute and whole. As I write these words it strikes me this is how Life loves us — absolutely and wholly times infinity. *Sam can count on me; I will be there with him to the end, come thick or thin.* Just as Life is there for us.

Even in uncertain times.

18

SURRENDER OFTEN

sometimes
you have to
surrender,
and curl into
life's turnings

trust the seasons,
trust the cycles,
trust our hearts
to grow in learning
shape shifting
slip sliding
song singing
soul shaping,
blades of grass
swaying —

in an emerald breeze
simply allowing
what will be to be,
forever leaning
into life's
possibilities

surrendering
to a space of
field's
green
grace

19

OTHER SIDE

*W*hen we release and let go, there is always new life and new gifts on the other side.

That doesn't mean there won't be bumps, grief, hurt, and heartaches throughout the process. It doesn't mean life won't tip sideways during the change and throw curveballs at us.

It just means, on a fundamental level, when we yield to life and try and lean into the change — there will always be new life and love waiting.

20

THE FIELD, PART II

I had a dream this afternoon Sam and I were sitting in a field of roses, on a big blanket in the center, as butterflies and ladybugs joyfully flew overhead. It was so magical and divine, I knew it as a message of love as there was only love there, and I hope to return to that field again whether by land of dream, heart, or imagination.

Sam passed away last Monday. We had hoped for six more months with him, and instead, we got one last month.

It happened so suddenly. One Tuesday all was fine, and we enjoyed going up to our magical field in Kokee State Park for a picnic, afternoon of cloud gazing, and creating a precious memory for his last summer. Then the next day he wasn't fine.

He went downhill fast.

We knew it was his time, so we took him to the ocean once more before we had to say goodbye.

Even as a grief author, I've found myself at a loss to convey the depth of what I'm feeling or the nature of our relationship. Though perhaps anybody who has been lucky enough to be blessed with the love of a sweet old dog already knows the depth and nature of which I speak.

They say those who have cancer travel close to God, and I figure this must be true of Sam as there was something so pure and angelic about him, he always felt otherworldly. He was the guardian angel of our family and inhabited the deepest and softest part of our hearts.

Now I've found myself on a new grief passage, learning new grief lessons I don't really feel like experiencing or learning. Recent years have brought a lot of loss into my life, and I'm tired of losing.

Nobody ever wants to take a grief passage; they are never convenient and rarely welcome. That doesn't matter to grief though — it simply appears in its own time, and we find ourselves unwittingly in its embrace. Grief comes in and rearranges us, and I've learned to offer myself up for the rearranging.

I believe anybody who takes a grief journey has embarked upon a holy journey.

Grief work is sacred work. Though often messy and dark, it is the kind of work that goes beyond our day-to-day and takes us into other realms, lands, and emotional vistas — we travel far outside the bounds of ordinary reality when we grapple with grief.

This is the space where we will feel splintering pain and begin to truly understand the depths of our own hearts. It is also the space where transcendence and transformation intersect, and we have the potential to realize the enduring effects of love, while discovering a greater breadth of spiritual truths.

I believe this is one of the reasons much of the grief experience is hard to put words to. Grief encompasses both the abyss and the heavens; our lowest lows and our highest highs. Such experiences defy language and are usually best understood within the space of our heart and soul.

I'm feeling things about Sam, which I am not able to put words to at present.

Even as life swirls on and I am making myself move forward to try and embrace gifts of day, there is a part of myself who has retreated into a secret place inside. It's a holy place where I grieve and honor our relationship, even as I still feel and sense Sam with me and marvel at spirit's grace and love's endurance.

I am an afterlife believer. I've been writing about feeling my brother in the afterlife for quite a while, so it's not a question of believing if Sam's spirit is close by or if I'll see him again. I am sure my dream was a blessing from Sam, along with the many synchronicities that have occurred over the past few days, which assure me he is free, safe, and truly our angel dog now.

My grief isn't tangled up with questions about where he went. It is tangled up in the missing. The physical missing. The beauty of our earthly life. The gift of his presence in our family which helped anchor our home.

Next week will mark our first full year on Kauai. There is sorrow in my heart as I write these words — Sam was supposed to be a part of the celebration. Yet there is also tender acknowledgment

Sam will always be a part of the celebration and hold a special place of honor in our family. *He was the family member with the biggest heart.*

It feels like Sam left us midstream, though perhaps he fulfilled his purpose of loving our family well and seeing us through this first year of change.

We sat in that field today, him and I, in dream-space, watching the tulips sway and receiving the blessings of the butterflies. They remind me change is life's way and all cocoons will give way to new wings.

I don't quite know how my new wings will look. Or what I'll do without my Sam. Or what the start of year two in Kauai will hold.

I do know I have another sweet pup at my side, who has been glued extra close. Frodo and I climbed our favorite mountain this morning and sat at the top, staring out at the blue, green, and vast spans of ocean. Thinking about life, thinking about Brent, thinking about how Kauai is home.

Thanking Sam inside my heart for helping make it such a good home this first year.

Somewhere in another realm close by, a little white dog, who's earned his angel wings, ran with us to the top, sparkling like the stars, romping through fields of pink roses along the way.

21

MANY WATERS

she is many
waters and oceans,
not all of them
explored

some can only
be accessed
by moonlight
and grief's
portal —

entry
only granted
where love
and loss
meet

brightest pearls
only formed
when heart
swims sea's
deep

22

What Spirit Said on Moon

*T*he moon is a reflection of all the change going on right now. Even as she changes right before your eyes, you are going to find your lives changing right before your eyes.

For some of you that may constitute big shifts in your inner life and for some that will mean radical changes in external circumstances.

This is a time when things may happen so fast, they feel like they leave you reeling. But take a cue from the moon and try to embrace the cyclical nature of life, trusting that anything which appears to be disappearing or dissolving is simply an end of a cycle so something new can birth through and move towards fruition.

Focus on what's right in front of you or you're going to be pulled into too many energy eddies. Like getting sucked into other's twisters who pull you into their swirl — it makes it harder for you to see your path and have a sense of clarity.

You need to trust in your own journey and your ability to channel and transmit this information. Trust it is your legacy and your right to do so.

If you can keep your eyes focused on your heart purpose, while simply praying for humanity (instead of being sucked into things and being derailed) you'll stay clearer on your own vision.

Remember even Jesus didn't make everybody happy or do enough to please some! So, breathe. Focus on your heart. Focus on your purpose. Let the moon be your guide, who teaches you all faces are part of the whole and everything is not always as it seems.

23

HANALEI BAY

*T*he sun is setting in Hanalei Bay, and I'm wading in the waters, pretending to frolic and kick the sudsy foam.

I'm building a new website and my web-designer recommended I get photos: *BethAnne you are your brand, so it would be good to put a face with your name.* Being in front of the camera is not the most comfortable thing for me, but this is the second part of the day's shoot and the beautiful water, sunset sweeps, and camaraderie I've developed with the photographer relaxes me.

It's July 10th, the anniversary of the evening we left Alaska, and it's an auspicious date. I feel like I'm holding an ocean of emotion inside of me. I'm viscerally aware of my memories of our last day in Anchorage one year ago, all that's transpired since, and the freshness of suddenly losing Sam.

Last year I remember exhaustion mixed with relief, a life deconstructed, a lot of stress, and one final push to wrap all loose ends up before getting on the final flight. We departed the day after the full moon in Capricorn. I would later learn the asteroid Vesta, who represents home, heart, and hearth, was in perfect conjunction with my natal Vesta at the exact point it sits my star chart that particular night, as if spirit was winking at me and letting me know the stars were magically aligned.

This year feels less starry, and I find myself taking pictures in the surf, contemplating a life still under construction, feeling swirls of deep grief, and stepping into a sense of wonder and deeper integration of Kauai being home.

Kauai IS home. I affirm this to myself as the light changes, and we play with shadow and water in the pictures. It's still a new home in many ways, and this summer I've struggled with missing my old space of self and feeling jaded over the hardship of our first year on the island.

People often focus on the courage it takes to take a leap of faith, but they don't always talk about what happens after you land. How great it will initially feel to have a sense of terra firma underneath you again. How disorienting it can be when you realize you have no idea how to navigate an entirely new terrain. How exhilarating it is to have the opportunity for reinvention.

How discouraging it is when things don't come together like you thought they would. How many crises of self you'll likely go through as your soul goes through deep process work. How you tunnel deeper into your relationship with yourself, and with spirit, as you work through each crisis and keep moving ahead with an open heart.

I'm trying to keep moving forward with an open heart.

I found a tuft of Sam's hair in my purse earlier in the day, right after we wrapped up the morning part of the shoot. We had just finished trucking through the mud into a forest of giant mahogany trees where the light streamed through. I talked to the trees in my mind to stay grounded and made sure Frodo was included in plenty of the pictures.

I was nervous on the drive over. I feel so tender and vulnerable with Sam gone. It turns out it was good for me to be pulled out of my grief cave, because it invited me into the present moment, reminded me of my dreams for the future, and helped me focus on building my new business.

When I found that soft tuft of fur it felt like a comfort message from Sam, *I know you miss me mom, but I'm still right here with you.*

I drove to the beach with a lighter heart for the evening part of the shoot. I'm wearing my favorite dress, hair up in my signature messy bun, and I feel like me. I brought all my books to capture in the photos and even that feels life-affirming. I look at them and count six, with another one soon on the way. It makes me take in the moment and realize how hard and how long I've been working on my dreams.

I've been the patient artesian. Getting better at what I do the longer I practice. Hunched over the workbench in my shop, carefully chiseling, hammering, and refining. Sometimes my work has been interrupted, but I've always returned to my workbench.

I try and receive and recognize what I've achieved, instead of focusing on how far I still feel I have to go.

A couple down the beach is getting married as the ocean gently laps and the sky turns peach. We are close enough to catch their joy, which is infectious, and the rest of the shoot unfolds with a sense of happiness and play.

I stare at the golden sky and think about how far I've come since we left Alaska one year ago. I think about how much I miss Sam and how sad, beautiful, and strange life is with its never-ending cycles of death and rebirth. I think about my own rebirth; what I'm trying to bring into the world, how far I've come, how far I feel I still have to go.

As with any act of creation, there's been chaos and collapse, which has slowly allowed for new form. Landing after a leap isn't always easy, but there's much potential for growth and becoming as you learn to find your way.

The sky slowly melts into honeyed apricots, and I have a sense of resonance and affirmation: *I am here, living this change and finding my way through the process. Come what may I'm still grateful to call Kauai home and continue to learn to be more like the ocean.*

Fluid, changeful, a force to be reckoned with, receptive, allowing, and free.

24

LAVENDER PAINT

You have to release people to Life.
Again and again, then some more.

Starting with yourself
and your expectations for how
you thought you would look,
who you thought you would be,
how you expected your life to go.

After all, even the wisest trees
don't know quite how tall, wide
or far they'll grow.

There is so much mystery in this space,
we don't have to solve it
to experience its grace.

Letting ourselves be shaped
by soil's mahogany deep
and sky's lavender paint —

Releasing the need to manage control,
and instead radically allowing
our change.

Knowing all that matters most
is the love we create in our days.

25

POTATO CHIPS AND PINK STONES

I'm eating potato chips in bed in my blanket fort. The lawn guy is here, and I'm hiding out, because words are too hard to form; I've been about 50 different people since this morning and my two teaspoons of energy are all used up.

Grief will do that to you, its disintegrating effects leaving you in fragmentation.

One-minute stable. The next undone. Then having a panic attack at the dairy aisle — plain or flavored, flavored or plain?! My brain cannot decide, and I buy potato chips instead.

I thought something might be wrong with my chest, but I realized my heart has splintered again and there's not enough rose quartz to put my chakra back in place.

What they don't tell you about grief work is grief is more than just making peace and coming to terms with those who've passed.

Overarching the grief journey is the bigger work of coming to terms with Life. You can't really come to terms with your grief and make peace with what you've lost if you don't do the bigger work of coming to terms with Life.

Grief shakes up, shakes out, shakes down everything you thought you believed.

Grief rearranges in its totality.

It will leave you tossing and turning at 3 a.m. and dreaming impossible dreams, whose possibilities become the seeds by which you keep breathing.

It leaves you driving down the highway, clutching your heart, feeling your neurons in disarray trying to make sense of nonsense.

There is no conclusion to its irresolution though some vague part of my memory keeps whispering "this will pass."

It won't pass in the night. Or on its own accord. Or swiftly. Mostly likely as time goes by, you'll notice the ache in your chest may begin to ease. Your mind will slowly sort and reorganize itself. Your tilted reality may not feel right, but you'll learn to walk sideways and see the world differently than those walking around uninitiated by grief.

Maybe you'll wander into a crystal shop. Buy a piece of rose quartz. Hide it in plain sight in the hopes another sideways walker will come along and find it like a cairn of pink hope, in a world that often feels less than light. So, they can be reminded:

All things will mend with love in time.

26

TREE BRAILLE

Sundays are
for silence;
for sounds of
malachite soul
and belonging to
the forest thick
and deep.

I hide myself
among her needles
of aged old pines,
and they tell me
overexposure
is far overrated —

It is better to stand
where you are planted
and simply allow
yourself time
to take root
and find
your wise.

We understand
each other
— I and the trees —
each of us
tucking our
bottomless
vulnerability
beneath a sage
visage of
mossy rings and
braille-laced
bark.

If you press your
hands against us long
enough, you'll
read-feel-see
the same
stories:

Ground in Love.
Stand in Love.
Reach in Love.
Grow in Love.

27

Moving Forward

*Y*ou don't have to move forward. Moving forward is a choice, not a requirement.

Sometimes staying in the same place can be a good thing. Staying in the same space isn't always stuck. Staying in the same space is sometimes a break or pause or rest. It's getting a quarter of the way along the trail, knowing you have a way to go, and judiciously taking a respite, allowing yourself time to breathe and reflect before you get up and begin taking those next few steps.

Grief. Trauma. Heartache. The hard stuff. We don't like to see people uncomfortable, it's hard for us. So, these are all areas in our lives where it will be more comfortable for other people to see us move forward than stay where we are at.

And they may not understand why you appear to be in the same place.

But they are not you. They may not know that your lungs are almost empty and it's going to take you a while to fill them back up. Or that something is cracked or broken and you're going to have to find healing where you are at, before you find what you need to move forward. Or that you simply are not ready. That is okay.

Moving forward is a choice and one you should choose when your heart feels ready and you realize it's not serving you to stay in the same spot.

When you realize you've filled your lungs up and healed your cracks as much as you can from your current vantage point. When you realize the only way to find bigger breaths is to begin to get up and walk, so you can clear the muggy thick of the trees. When you realize you can't find deeper healing in your current space of self — because you're only going to transcend that space if you stretch beyond and venture forth.

When you realize those things, you know you're being called to move.

You'll know the sunlight is beckoning you, asking you to receive its medicine of hope. You'll know life has new gifts waiting if you dare to release and step into new terrain. You'll know you'll never forget where you have been, but it now feels okay to think about where you'll like to go.

Most of all you'd know your own pace of self and process of movement is humanly, divinely, imperfectly perfect for you.

28

SALT

On a muggy, slow Saturday I find myself biking along the Kapaa bike path. Right by the ocean, the views of the aquamarine water and craggy coastal rocks are spectacular. The humidity and sea salt are so strong here, I notice my new silver bracelet — *Baby Bear* is engraved on it in memory of my Samwise — has tarnish marks. The elements have a way of overtaking things and changing them in accord.

They've changed me too.

I remember biking along this same path last year. Everything was new and shiny. It was a novelty to be on a cruiser bike, chugging along with Frodo in the basket, wheels churning over and over as I kept marveling at the truth: *This is my new home!*

I'd smile cheerfully at the tourists out on their rental bikes. Wave to others using the path; some wave back, some don't. Kapaa is a strange mix of characters. Mostly the ocean captured my gaze — ever reaching spans of marine set against salty blue sky — and I felt enchanted by this beautiful island and the fact I had found the courage and guts to move here.

The thing about being enchanted is, as life churns along, it's difficult to live in a space of enchantment, because it's not real.

In fact, at some point in any kind of relationship, including the space we call home, we will most likely go through a period of disenchantment and disillusionment, as we work towards a deeper, more authentic, more knowing relationship.

I find myself in this space now, as I grieve and work on letting go and accepting Sam's loss. I reflect on this past year as I pedal along the coastal trail, Frodo once again ensconced in my basket, the sea lending itself to introspection and revelry.

I think about the strange construct of time and how long a year can be, yet how short a year can be: Kauai is, in many ways, still brand new. We've transplanted here and planted new seeds, but those seeds have barely taken root. Our life is still half-formed and not exactly where I thought it would be within a year's time.

I had great expectations, and when expectations are not met, we tend to get frustrated and disillusioned with life. Sam's illness and quick departure at the beginning of July thrust me into a space of chaos, conflict, pain, evaluation, and disillusion. Admittedly, grief is the origin of all of this — one can't go through grief without having to deal with feeling disillusioned over life or without feeling the pain which comes from loving and losing.

But my grief has also cast a pall on everything else and left me questioning my purpose and journey, wondering if I've missed the mark. I believed things would magically and effortlessly line up when I moved to Kauai and that's not how the past year shaped up.

I expected after taking my leap of faith, it would take several months to find firm footing on the island and to begin to find a new place and new direction. The truth is that it's been a year and I'm still working on that firm footing.

It strikes me after I leapt, I landed in a brand-new land with a brand-new heart language and brand-new sense of self. It's a lot of new territory to navigate. When I throw in the change from extraneous variables outside of myself, which I've had no control over, I've been knocked off balance even more.

I've kept finding what I felt was firm footing this past year only to find things tilt again.

I notice my bike tilting, somewhere in the middle of my reflections, and I realize it's become more difficult to pedal up the small hill I'm cruising. I pull over and upon further investigation see my tires are low and almost flat, and I begin to walk the bike back to my car, Frodo still enjoying the slow push in the basket, the crash of salt-seas waves having a Zen-like effect on him.

The symbolic irony of last summer's rides of ease and joyful thoughts compared to this summer's unexpected flat and my musings on disillusionment does not escape me. Sometimes life has an absurd sense of humor, and while I'm not laughing with it, I haven't totally lost perspective that despite our best efforts and most beautiful thoughts, life is a force all its own and it likes to tip sideways and surprise us.

I've been surprised before. I know I'm going to have to keep trying to find ways to reach through my grief and grow through my sense of disillusionment and compression.

It's a long walk as I push my bike along those coastal trails, grateful for my sunglasses when I realize salt-laden tears are slowly streaming down my face. I'm not even sure what I'm crying for: Sam? My confused sense of home? Unmet expectations? Life's corkscrews and loops that deposited me somewhere other than where I expected, leaving me flat.

The full of life can be so terribly wonderful and so wonderfully terrible. We find ourselves in the mix doing our best to make sense of it in a way that serves us and carries us forward.

I keep pushing forward that day, tear-stained cheeks, salt-stained bracelet, love-stained heart.

I miss my Sam; I miss the shine of last year's brand new. Yet somewhere inside of me I intuitively know this is still where I'm meant to be. I haven't messed up and life hasn't messed up, and all the beautiful possibilities meant to be are still seeding, growing, and waiting to expand into new formation.

There's hope on the horizon, I can't quite feel it or see it, but I have to remember it's waiting and try to keep belief. For today, I keep up my slow push along the path, looking down, noticing the coast and the way the elements, corrode, erode, rearrange, and relieve. Looking up, tilting my face to the sky's salt breeze.

29

The Beautiful Mess

*I*f it's messy and awkward and experience laden with a lot of course corrections and re-navigations, then you're probably living life in a way where you're engaged in your growth and development, and what a beautiful thing.

Maybe it doesn't look neat or linear or well packaged and that's perfectly alright. People are so hard on themselves for being human, instead of recognizing how hard it is to be human and how hard it can be to embody our space of self. After all, what a splendid yet difficult journey it is to learn to navigate our unique mix of mind, body, heart, and spirit and how that translates and transforms with our experiences.

It's a lot.

So, go gently. Find grace for your process. Empower yourself to keep taking responsibility for all parts of you as you go about the work of navigating and mapping out your territory of self. Forgive often. Learn to laugh at the inelegant moments and see them for the growing pains they are as you stretch and reach and learn to be bigger.

Do you. And learn that while some things we do may require apology (mistakes are part of life and repair work is necessary and healing), one thing you never have to apologize for is figuring yourself out and giving yourself permission to take the inner journey into a deeper you.

30

AUGUST HAZE

*T*he summer is thick and syrupy right now. Humidity drips from the trees, and there's a heaviness to the jungle air, which going to the ocean relieves. August has come with a density of energy, which both stills and quickens a deepening sense of mystery.

July passed in a blink.

A month of solar and lunar eclipses, I was left with the feeling life was transforming and shifting around me, yet it all felt eclipsed by the pain in my heart.

July was shadowed with grief over losing Sam, and grief's undertow has a way of taking one down the river to places you didn't expect to go. It can take a while to swim upstream and get back on track.

Or to let the water carry you until you find yourself washed out and up onto new ground and you find a new track.

It occurred to me the other day I've been reorienting myself and finding a new track since the day my brother died. Brent was the catalyst for pulling up all my roots and transplanting to Kauai, and though I think I would have still made this move eventually, I can say with certitude that losing him pushed me to do it Now, and not wait until Later.

Here I am Now. It's been a little over a year, and as I take in the whole of the year, there's reflections and lessons and learnings I couldn't see in the middle.

But I can see them now.

Like gazing at individual stars compared to widening our gaze and taking in an entire constellation; we can't always see the bigger picture when we're focusing on the smaller pieces. There is value to be found in both perspectives.

I've spent a lot of this past year retrieving, collecting, and actualizing new pieces. There wasn't much space for them in my

Anchorage life, there is here. It's been a process both exhausting and exhilarating. It is a process that is still ongoing.

Having passed the year mark, I'm better able to see a fuller picture of what those pieces are building, and it's a fuller picture of my multifaceted self with more room for all parts of me. I'm also coming to see I've been discovering —

A deeper understanding of home.

A deeper appreciation for my life and a wiser understanding of how losing Brent inextricably changed me and set me on a life path with more room for authenticity, magic, and love.

An unmasked self who keeps learning in bigger and greater ways to stand strong in her gifts and power.

Becoming is a process. One in which we'll be engaging our entire lives. There are no timelines or deadlines or any lines other than the lines of self we learn to trace as we learn to navigate our map of self.

We will forever be a work in progress finding ourselves in bits and pieces, retrieving our truths along the way. And I am grateful to be here, doing just that. Finding myself, going into my second year in Kauai, continuing to unmask and become —

Stepping into a fuller self beneath the grace of these hazy August days.

31

How to Mend

Sometimes you just
have to forgive this life
for being what it is:
Imperfect.

For failing to support
you in the places
you thought you
needed support,
and for revealing to you
the places where
you didn't even know
you'd begun to crack —

So, you can learn
where
why
and how
you need to mend.

It's not easy,
staying open to your
heart when it's easier to
close, but it is
worth it if you want
to live a life
transcending complacency,
ripe with vivacity
defying mediocrity,
complex with curiosity —

Then my dear one
you have to forgive
what did and didn't
happen:

(finding radical acceptance for this process called life)

And gift yourself the gift
of a free heart,
so, you can keep
moving forward
in love.

32

DEAR MOM, YOUR SAM

Dear Mom,

You will feel these words more than you will hear them, if you close your eyes and drop into your heart, you will feel me and what I want to tell you.

See me with your heart. I'm right here. Next to you.

Know it's a sign from me when you see a ladybug, or a pink rose. I'm going to give you a pink rose today. Pay attention for it.

I'm learning about unconditional joy now. Let me help you feel the joy too. Focus on your heart and you'll feel me and my joy.

I might come back someday, but not yet. I need to be here right now, in the joy, supporting you with my joy.

I'm always close by. I am always a part of your home. Thank you for all the love.

Your Sam

33

SOPHOMORE YEAR

*T*he Summer of 2018 was nothing like I thought it would be. I believe I will forever remember it as the summer of disillusionment and forced soul growth, where losing Sam became the catalyst for reevaluating my sense of purpose, my relationship to the island, and my attachment to the idea of home.

Back in the spring, I was anticipating a summer of expansion and growth, and I had no idea I was about to go through another grief journey and contract into a space of heartache and depression. The whole summer I've felt some part of myself dampened, confused, and pressed down upon, even as I try and move forward.

I come back to myself slowly. It takes time. Sam has left me bruised and tender, and there is a nameless grief inside.

I move haltingly through the days, but I do move. I work on getting content together for a new website. I set up an online space to teach and begin working on creating a free course, which challenges and stretches me to grow professionally.

I turn 41 on the day of an Aquarius full lunar eclipse, and I think about what I'd like the upcoming year to bring. I polish up my children's book and set the release date for September. *Transformations of The Sun* comes out, and I try and appreciate publishing another book and celebrating the moment.

I do these things in bits and pieces, small spurts and occasional sprints. Some days it's hard to get out of bed, I nap a lot and my energy is low.

I try though, I try to move forward. I can feel some part of me resisting all the change. She doesn't want to move forward; she wants to wallow in missing Sam and stay in the memory of those last weeks with Sam. She wants to go back to life when it felt simpler and less complex and her gravitational orbit felt more centered.

Maybe there's even some part of myself who is afraid to create new memories, because creating new memories means moving on, and moving on means leaving behind what's come to pass.

I'm so tired of letting go, my heart hurts in exhaustion.

Sometimes it makes me so very sad when I consider how much I've been asked to release in a short period: Brent, Alaska, Sam. There are layers and layers of letting go composed within each. Yet, I also look around me at the muggy jungles and thick hibiscus bushes, and I know I would never be here if I was somebody who allowed herself to cling to the past.

On a soul level, I know the love remains, which means the love I've held for everything which has passed is still carried in my heart, still nourishing me and growing my heart stronger.

I try and make peace with the island and make peace with how our first year spun out. *Messy, difficult, transformative — human.*

I try and think about my relationship with Kauai as any intimate relationship, because all intimate relationships go through periods of disillusionment, reconciliation, and growth. I work on realizing disillusionment is the opportunity to accept something on a deeper level — the diamonds and the flaws — and find a greater acceptance for the truth of the whole.

I try and shift my perspective, so I embrace my changeful relationship with Kauai as an impetus to a more intimate relationship with myself. The upheaval of this summer has forced me to go digging and sifting for my gold again, yet I'm finding my inner work helps ground me even deeper into my sense of self and sense of internal wisdom.

Sorting, filtering, and examining value systems, expectations, and beliefs about life will always help us spiral back into ourselves and realize, reaffirm, and reorganize our truths on a deeper level than before.

I've sat with myself a great deal this summer. I've sat with home. I've sat with Sam. I've sat with my sense of greater purpose and how my purpose intersects with just being human. Mostly I've sat with the island, working out the knots and kinks in my relationship with her vast visage of change.

I let Mother Kauai's ocean teach me about letting go and moving forward; she says she does it all the time, and I can too. She surrounds me in my visions and reminds me I know how to swim in the deep end. She reminds me my island of self is constantly being shaped and formed by the tides and waves of Life's Sea.

I go to her often and try to embody her wisdom letting my feelings and grief flow and release as she speaks:

Life isn't linear. It's cyclical. Fluid, flowing, ebbing, growing. Constantly moving us along.

There is value in letting go and trusting the deeper knowledge of soul will come in time. You don't have to work so hard to figure everything out or effort away at life, you just have to trust in your own pace, process, rhythm, and growth.

So, my dear girl, stop resisting. Embrace what is. Learn to lean into my waves of change, surrender, and flow.

Earth Below Me

The sun does
not seek out
another to
teach it how
to be a light.

34

UNRAVELINGS

The emerald breeze
she gathers me,
she's become an old
friend,
who knows my needs.

No longer as new
as she used to be,
there is
a depth
a compatibility
a familiarity
a history.

She's watched me
grow,
just like her trees,
new roots laid down
in Kauai's
green.

New arms outstretched
towards sky's luminosity
— still intrinsically me —
I've also
become
more like she:

Patient,
gracious,
more expectation-free
...we shift shapes
and grow deeper
through life's
unravelings.

Returning
within
every time we
sieve —

*old husks of self
giving way to
new leaves.*

35

MARATHON

*T*he first day of September begins with the Kauai Marathon. I'm a reluctant participant in this year's race. A yearly marathon is a way of life in our household — we met at mile 7.5 in the Silver Falls Marathon, so it's in our blood — but my heart isn't in it.

After my rough summer, my energy is down, my adrenals are fatigued, I'm just now emerging from my grief laden depression and have only done the bare minimum to prepare for the race. Most of my long training runs have been slow, frustrating, and ended with me breaking down crying on the trail.

It's been a rough season for my husband too who navigated the loss of Sam while juggling job difficulties and work stress. We've been struggling with transition in our personal journeys and our journey as a couple since we've been on this island. Household morale has, at times, been low.

We signed up for the race though, and despite neither of us feeling like our best running selves, it's not in our natures to throw in the towel without at least trying.

When the alarm goes off at 4:30 that morning, I'm relieved I was able to sleep. I don't feel like the energizer bunny, but I don't have the feeling I've been battling since we lost Sam where I'll feel like I'm going to fall asleep walking, because my body is so fatigued. I check in with myself and decide that today I feel like a car with just enough gas in the tank to get the job done.

It's dark when we get to Poipu. There's the usual pre-race frenzy of checking to make sure we have any needed nutrition, lightly jogging to wake our legs up, negotiating the huge throng of people participating and spectating, then getting ourselves situated at a reasonable place at the start line.

A special aloha blessing is given, the sound of the conch shell echoes the start of the race, and I start running.

Being a marathoner can teach you a lot about life. There's a certain mindset that comes with the knowledge you have 26.2 miles to go. It's helped that I've done other endurance races, which were farther in distance, because I can always draw on those memories to motivate and remind myself of my capability. But for where I'm at in life right now, 26.2 miles is plenty. I'm just grateful to find my energy feeling reasonably up to the task.

The first 7–8 miles pass slow and steady. The sun starts fully coming up in the sky around mile 9, it begins to get hot, and my foot starts to hurt. I ignore it and do my mental trick of trying to focus on other things.

At mile 10, it's tempting to cut left instead of right. Given my rocky training runs, my husband and I had already discussed I would give myself an out if I felt my adrenals crashing and didn't think I could complete the race. Left is where the half marathoners are headed, soon to be done with their race. Right is the out and back loop for the marathoners, which consists of a long slog of hills and heat.

I go right. It is a slog. I'm not at my best, but I am capable, though slow, as I run on the hot pavement, stopping occasionally at an aid station for a needed glass of water or orange slice. The only thing remarkable to share about the next few miles is I begin to see the fastest runners already looping back. I'm amazed at their physicality and contemplate how we are all in the same race, yet skillset and abilities vary so much.

Right around mile 14, which takes place on this huge, horrible hill winding up into a neighborhood in a town called Kaleho, I notice one of the fast runners coming my way. What is only mile 14 for me, is mile 20 for him — I've still got a lot more hill to go up, then a bunch of ups and downs which will loop me back around before I'll find myself running back down this same hill.

What is magical about this runner coming my way is that he's my husband. Eric is running the fastest I've ever seen him. He stops to give me a quick kiss, not knowing how well he's actually doing, and I find myself tearing up as I say, *Run, run! You're in 8th place right now, you're one of the fast ones today! Run Eric run!*

It carries me for the next few miles.

It's not been easy for us on the island. Eric's had a difficult time finding good work. We've had a lot of ups and downs individually and as a couple, which has challenged us to develop a new sense of personal identity and marital identity. Then Sam died on top of all of that changing the nucleus of our family.

We'd agreed before the race start, we needed a win as a family, and I knew we'd get one today. Eric is running the best race of his life.

My race is less remarkable. As I write these words, I remember a lot of hot. Sweat. Pain. Perseverance. It was one of my slower years, and I walked more than I usually do. The last 3 miles seemed endless. A long-suffering stretch of digging deep and reminding myself I once did an Ironman; I can complete this marathon.

I stayed with myself, stayed with my thoughts, my tired legs, kept moving forward, sometimes a bit faster, sometimes a bit slower, inching closer to the end. It was a relief when I crossed, and finally got to sit down, take water, allow my mental fortitude to dissolve and shift into post-race relaxation mode.

Eric receives his medal for placing in his age group and finds out he did finish 8th, putting in the fastest marathon time he's ever had on the hardest course we've run. The day wasn't about numbers for me, just appreciation and gratitude. I did it and my body carried me the distance.

More so though, the day is about getting our feet back under us again after a summer that knocked us down. *It is about remembering we do belong to this island and are literally supported by the ground beneath our feet.*

It is about celebrating Eric's victory, which he considers a family victory, and finding joy in the joint accomplishment of both completing the race. Afterwards, we languish on the couch at home with snacks and relaxation, with a dog who is very happy to see us.

The day is about continuing to be open to our new home and realizing our definition of home is still evolving, and so are we. It is about returning to ourselves through the familiar act of running — something that's anchored us since the day we met.

Running is a bridge that always allows us to cross any territory and return to the truth of who we are. So many truths have changed, but the core of who we are remains. It feels good to acknowledge our truth and keep allowing ourselves to be changed by the island as we run towards a new season.

36

September Goals

*G*race. Ease. Tangible Steps. Stay in my lane. Try to observe and learn from my reactions to others, but don't be overly concerned by their paths. Do me instead.

Trust the universe actually is supporting me and working in my favor. If it feels like I'm having to effort at my relationship with the universe, stop efforting. Surrender often. *Remember the mystery is bigger than all this stuff I supposedly think I know, so just be a star adventurer and soul explorer and heart anthropologist.*

Teach those things. Stay open. Let go of anything that knocks me off my heart path, because that's where the real magic is at.

Create as much as I can. Remember I will have all the time I need to bring my creative dreams to fruition. Kindness and crystals. Grapple with the messy stuff. Let it be messy. Believe in my ability to learn and grow.

Listen to the tree songs. Keep my eyes open for fairies. Coffee and dog. Clarity and love. Let it be what it is and find the grace in that. Always bring the magic.

37

CONSCIOUS RECEPTIVITY

"The most beautiful experience we can have is the mysterious.
It is the fundamental emotion that stands at the cradle of
true art and true science."
— ALBERT EINSTEIN

A new awareness has been dawning inside of me. It began the other day while I was at the ocean. I was watching the aquamarine waves, the contented people on the beach, and then time seemed to still in that moment, as if everything is in slow motion.

There is an ease to the water and an ease to the energy. I have the strangest sense I'm on the cusp of understanding something much bigger than myself, though I can't fully grasp what. I can feel it though. In that moment, I begin to sense, perceive and feel how much grace and space opens up when we move with life's energy instead of against it.

What happens next — on the golden beach, by the blue ocean, in the crystalline moment — is something I can't fully convey in writing. I'm going to try however, because it creates a critical turning point in how I understand energy and how the universe works.

A vision appears in my mind of a beautiful field filled with sparkling, glistening particles of energy. They are sentient, electric, alive. I intuitively sense it is source energy, the material the universe is made of and it's trying to show me something about itself.

I begin to intuitively feel that we can consciously pull this energy towards ourselves when we keep our hearts open and set our intentions with clarity. Never one to think overly much on concepts like manifestation, I suddenly have the new thought in my mind that *this* is how we manifest:

We draw energy from our hearts into our auric field and being, so the energy has a clear place to enter the pattern of our lives, land, and begin to help us materialize our intentions and dreams in tangible ways.

What is astounding about my vision is the love, peace and *neutrality* I can feel in the glistening energy field. It doesn't feel like anyone is up there monitoring and meting it out based on good or bad behavior. It is unconditional in nature: equally available to each of us. We just have to know how to work with it and call it into our lives.

My unexpected, transcendent beach experience marks the origins of a profound shift in my consciousness. I begin to understand that if we invite energy (Spirit, God, Higher Power, the Universe — however we understand the nature of the divine) into the spaces we've created in our lives, we can create greater space for growth and actualization.

I begin to understand resistance limits energy. If we don't resist the moment, and instead open our hearts and say, "I invite you to come in and help me work with this," we open up enormous space for Life to support us.

I begin to understand resisting the flow of life creates energetic blocks and density inside of ourselves, which creates an energetic traffic jam making it harder to move energy and manifest opportunity.

I begin to test this out. When challenges arise, I try and sink into them, trust, and ask life, "please come support me in this and create a good outcome from these circumstances." My car has issues. My computer crashes. Taxes are due and I'm stressed. Each time something happens, I spend time meditating and calling in help, ease, and grace.

I watch with interest as the pattern arranges itself around my circumstances: Unexpected money shows up. My husband spontaneously is given the day off, and his presence makes it easier to troubleshoot the double trouble day when the car acts up *and* the computer crashes. We end up having an unexpected lunch in Lihue as we wait for everything to be diagnosed. My dad steps in and surprises me with a new computer. I get my taxes in on time and instead of stress just feel relief and release.

The paradigm of how I understand life, spirit, and the universe begins to shift. It springs alive for me in an incredibly intelligent, loving, creative way, and I begin to understand I don't know half as much I think I know. I become a student all over again, and I begin to ponder on principles like allowance, receiving, and exactly how life unfolds.

I now understand I had a lot of expectations surrounding how I thought my life was going to look when I first moved to Kauai, and I wasted a great deal of energy attaching to and interpreting what it meant that my expectations weren't occurring (which is all good, because just another heart lesson, right?). I also begin to truly understand what it means to surrender and let go of the *how*.

I am opening up. With curiosity and wonder. I realize there are whole levels, layers, and discoveries waiting for me when I truly receive from life instead of dictating to life. I understand now resistance limits energy, so I'm trying to stay open to my life, keep aligning my intentions, and allow my process to unfold.

Kauai is teaching me that bringing desires to fruition is entirely possible even if we can't see the way. That if we take the time to dream it and nourish the seeds of our dreams with vision, intent and a good dose of asking the universe — "please bring me what I need to accomplish this" — things have a way of manifesting in time.

We can bring peace into our beings through intentional allowance, and in so doing we will create more space in our energetic field for life to come in and co-create. Open up to the pattern and direction of life, so we learn to trust it, stay with its rhythm, and dance with the cosmos in flow.

38

CREATIVE ADAPTATION

*P*atience is often difficult. There are many things we wanted to know yesterday, which we may not be any closer to knowing today. There are things we want to happen now, when the timing isn't there.

What a strange contradiction being human is: we often seek the stability that comes from knowing, as if knowing somehow gives us a sense of constancy — even though we all know that change IS the only constant.

And so, we have to find tiny anchors and pockets of shore which we can ground into to help create a sense of cohesion and solidity in the fluidity. We have to find ways to bring ourselves back to ourselves all while offering ourselves up to Life to be changed if we want soul growth. We have to find a way to make peace within the contradicting energies of movement and pause, knowing that balance is often overrated and unobtainable, but creative adaptation is a beautiful waltz.

Creative adaptation allows us to stay open to the possibilities and make art out of unexpected circumstances. To lean one way one day and then another way the next, and eventually learn that WE are the constant in the aventurine streams of life's flow. To become a co-participant in our creative process as we accept Life's grander invitation to create with it and make rainbows where darkness once lay.

To step into the mystic field and work with Spirit on levels deeper than we may have imagined, as we come to realize: perhaps what we thought we wanted to have happen Today, will be unimaginably better than anything we could have foreseen, when we let go, trust, and allow it space to happen in the Morrow.

Patience can be difficult. But it's also a necessity if we wish to receive the life of creative existence our hearts seek and are designed to be.

39

MESSAGE FROM THE BIRDS

birdsongs
on a wednesday
morn,
the jungle sways
and breathes
green warm

grace speaks
through nature's
sound and swarm,
sun shines down
and wisdom's
born

while a choir
of tweets
insists on sweetly
singing a chorus
of pinks and golds
and blues:

you have to learn
to tune out
the noise,
for it is only in
love's silence
that you will find
your deepest
truth

40

Everybody Has an Instrument

*L*ittle Sister, you have to try and not take things so personally. I know it feels personal and it's meant to be so you can experience and grow — but in the big scheme of things, so much of it is a show. People do what they think is expected of them to do. Most of them come into this world with a certain perspective and it's not yours to understand or change.

The trick is to separate the wheat from the chaff and learn to look more at the heart of people and less at the behavior. This is how you do this: *by examining the integrity of the instrument and getting past the noise it makes.*

Your job is to be a light bringer — so you help other people learn to see more clearly, which helps them examine the instruments, including their own.

Everybody is given an instrument when they come into this world and music they are called to create. Everybody has an instrument within their act of being and their soul can lead them and teach how to play. Except many don't understand this and they aren't really playing, or they don't know how to play the music they were designed to play.

(A rose can only bloom as big as the space it's allowed to bloom, don't stop pruning.)

Just keep doing what you're doing Little Sis, the rest will come in time. But you're already doing a good job helping people learn to play.

41

TERRA FIRMA

I don't know where the fall goes. I've lived it, I've breathed it.
I've loved it — this has been a season of joy, ease, and fluidity
which is a sigh of relief for my inner eco-system after the grief
and confusion of the summer.

September melts into October into November. A friend
comes to the island. We make memories of Poipu, Hanalei, and
hunting out great food trucks. I find new vision and confidence
to start crafting online courses, and I have a profound sense of
magic and pleasure as I weave my psychological, creativity, and
intuitive gifts together in new ways.

I buy candy corn for the two trick-or-treaters who stop by
our place. Our 4th wedding anniversary comes and goes. We eat
Italian and walk the dog on the beach and talk about our dreams.

I love this time of year. Autumn is my favorite season, and
while compared to most other places, Kauai doesn't have too much
of a fall, but if you pay attention autumn shows up in its own way.

It's a little cooler early in the morning, the guava berries are
dropping, some of the flowers fall away and close shop until
spring. The surf is higher, the light shifts, the sun rises a little later
further in the east and sets a little earlier further in the west.

There's a subtlety to the seasonal shift, and maybe that's what
I like. I like the quiet, the slight, the fine-spun evening light; the
small nuances that often go unnoticed. Paying attention causes
me to be stiller and keener. Perceive the in-betweens and soft
changes others miss.

There is a quiet transition going on that says: *even in Kauai,
the earth gets a wee bit sleepier this time of year, so new things can
later be reborn.*

I feel my own quiet transition happening while new things
begin to birth within. My profound shift at the beginning of

September has resulted in embracing, receiving, and working with the energy of spirit and universe in new, exciting ways.

I'm braver. More fearless. Answering lack with love. Inviting spirit into the spaces I've been creating to help grow them. Accepting how much I don't know and becoming a more authentic student of soul, as I allow my lessons to translate into my work.

Mostly, I feel space opening up inside of my heart, mind, and energy. I find the more I let go of how I thought things should be, the more I actually open to observing how they are. I realize I'm getting out of my own way, so I can experience bigger growth.

Autumn becomes a graceful space of flow. Mercury goes into retrograde, and in true retrograde fashion, I notice more of an inversion and slowing down of myself. Slightly cooler days slip into one another. The morning light sings with soft peaches, dusty roses, and pewter blues.

I realize after the tumult of last summer, which left me feeling I was being churned around in a stormy sea, that I have learned to ride the waves, and they've carried me to a new shore. *I'm standing on terra firma, and I have my feet underneath me again.*

I still miss Sam fiercely, but the pain doesn't stop my heart and sting in immediacy any longer. I take solace in a sense of his spirit and comfort in the fact I will never have to repeat losing him again and retrace those first horrible steps in the aftermath. I allow the locket hanging around my neck, with his picture and tuft of fur, to warm my heart and remind me love lives on inside our hearts.

I am on new ground, and I'm grateful and relieved. The grief of last summer enhances my appreciation for fall's flow and autumn's songs, and I receive and savor the grace of the season. *It's all the more reason to be a little bit cozy (candles, peppermint tea, an extra blanket on the bed), and let the flavors of nostalgia, pumpkin, and hearth ground me deeper into heart, earth, and home.*

42

Things I Learned Fall of '18

Musings, Perspectives, Insights & Affirmations from my Journal
{in no particular number or order}

1. Use your discomfort, your fears, and your doubts as tools for growth, so you can see where you're limiting yourself, then reach beyond that.

2. Don't allow other's fears to dictate your inner peace.

3. Create what you want to create, what's on your heart to create, and not what you think will sell or what you're expected to create. That's what true innovation is all about.

4. The beauty of what you're creating in Kauai is all intuitively based. It is heart directed and you can trust that. You can always trust your intuition and heart.

5. Learn to bring love into the spaces you fear.

6. You're meant to teach this: you are going to use your journey of transformation as a way to teach and empower others. It's just not quite time yet, you're still building the foundation.

7. Everything necessary for success is already within you. Keep inviting spirit into the spaces you are already touching.

8. However small a step, it is enough to get the ball rolling. Just keep taking steps and all else will flow.

9. Don't let somebody else's lack of faith in the universe become your own.

10. The universe will reflect back to you the story you believe and tell.

11. The universe loves a broken heart, because it means there's plenty of space to fill it with new light, love and life.

12. If the vision is coming from your heart then of course it is meant for you. Engaging in self-doubt is like betting against yourself, and why would you want to do that?

13. When in doubt make a list of teeny goals, so you stay on track and have a sense of movement, however small.

14. Your relationship to how you see this world is entirely your responsibility, so try and create thoughts which empower your growth. You create the paradigm for how you understand life and the universe, don't allow somebody else's structures to become your own if they are not living open-hearted and brave in this world.

15. There is little that a cup of mint tea won't calm and soothe.

16. Expectation limits spirit's playing field. The more we stay open to how our dreams will manifest, the greater opportunity there is for miracles and magic.

17. Your connection to the universe is your true source of abundance and nobody can take that from you.

43

Gemini Moon

The sun and moon
rest in perfect
equanimity.
Gemini rises
finding balance
through duality.

Where shadow
becomes light
and light becomes
dark, and dark
becomes the matter
to transform
our hearts.

The sky is endless
in cyclical reach;
teaching all phases
are valid and seen.
All sides of self
are the sum
of our full,
so, we must be
like the moon's
changeful soul.

Forever dissolving, revolving, evolving —
Finding our truth in the shades of our whole.

44

LEANING INTO THE UNKNOWN

I declared yesterday a soul-care day.

It's been a while since I've done an extreme day of self-love, and the other day, as I was writing a list of "soul-care activities" for a course, it occurred to me I should take my own advice and put it into practice. It's been a long, beautiful season of outward creative flow, and the quiet pause that comes with yuletide and the cusp of a new year offers the gift of breath, reflection, and turning inwards.

So, I decided to take advantage of that slowing, and I hopped in my car and let my whims lead. I felt drawn to stop at this little antique shop I've been eyeballing for months. Several charming purchases later — which included one awesome, 1964 antique metal milk-crate, from a Hawaiian farm that I was thrilled to find — I headed to the Southside for a bit of lunch, sun, and magic.

After living on Kauai for a year and a half, I've come to deeply appreciate how each side of the island has its own special eco-systems and gifts. There are flowers and trees on the southside you won't find anywhere else along with yellow and white butterflies, whose presence always make me feel like something magical is about to happen.

"Always sunny in Poipu" is a catchphrase often said, because though it might be raining in the northern and eastern jungles of the island, you can almost always find a spot of sun when you drive through the tree tunnel and head towards the southern tip. Lithified cliffs and turquoise seas make it an inviting beach destination, and I sunned and watched cliff jumpers while "best friend" (aka, Frodo) lay in the shade under a giant pine tree.

Mostly I spent yesterday in reflection.

It is Winter Solstice in the Northern Hemisphere, and even in Kauai there is a decrease in light, which lends itself to introspection, taking an inner walk through my chambers of self, and turning the lights on in each room to take stock of what's there. There's been a great deal of reshuffling and rearranging that's taken place. Moving to the island in 2017 was massive change, and I expected my next step and life path to form and foment quicker than what it did.

2018 turned out to be a building year. One where I've learned a lot about releasing expectation, developing extreme patience, showing up for myself and my dreams, and trusting in my relationship with Life in bigger ways. Mostly I've learned not to let somebody else's relationship with the Universe become my relationship with the Universe.

I choose to trust. To believe. To know I'll be supported by the innate, intelligence and creative force of Life, and I choose to root out any voices of fear and self-doubt that tell me otherwise.

I've learned to lean into the unknown in Kauai, and I spent quite a bit of time this last year challenging my own suppositions, lack-based beliefs, and just learning to be comfortable with not knowing. I've become a student all over again, and right around the time I realized how very little I actually know about the mysterious and beautiful force that is Life, I heard a voice speak clearly inside my mind, which said:

Oh good, you're figuring it out. And now that your mind is open — you're finally ready to teach.

So, I started creating online courses back in August and it's joyfully, and hard-work-fully, and delightfully consumed my days these past months. Toss in a new, professional website, the effort it took to write all the web content, and I've been in go mode for weeks: I have 3 courses out, a 4th one coming in February, and I don't know who or what I'll be after that or what exactly my work will be.

But that's life over here. Improvisational, fluid, creative, and free.

It's what I signed up for coming to Kauai. Sometimes that's been terrifying, but there is such beauty and naked vulnerability as well when I place myself in the creative flow of the mysteries and trust. Trust that if I show up each day, as best I know how, Life will meet me there and we'll create the next step together.

For now, I'm stepping quietly into year's end with plenty of space for rejuvenation, reflection, and releasing what has been, so

I can embrace what is. And today that means simple pleasures. A run in the sun. A trip to Orchid Alley to pick up a few new floral friends. Something good to eat. An afternoon on Donkey Beach — the tree tunnel to the ocean makes you feel like you're going through an enchanted portal, and the whales are out right now, so there's a good chance one may make an appearance while we beach.

A quiet evening spent on the couch in coziness, watching movies, just being, feeling grateful under the gaze of a bright, Full Cold Moon.

45

Burn

*I*t's the last day of 2018, and rain is pouring down in heavy sheets of gray. We've closed out the year well by spending our weekend doing celebratory adventures, reflecting on 2018, and preparing for 2019.

The last day of 2018 will be for a bit of tidying (because I like to go into the new year with a clean space), a run in the sun, then making intention lists before settling in for movies and good food with the fur kids. I'm looking forward to the intention lists, as they'll be a space to plant our dreams and seed our hopes for 2019.

It feels like a year for big change. I have a sense of anticipation inside, which has been building for a while. A felt sense that something big is coming. The fire in my heart, which I've stoked throughout the fall into a slow burn feels so close to being ready to let out and become a blaze *(though I'm not entirely sure what that even means)*.

I feel it however, and I've found our feelings are truths and premonitions, which we can intuitively sense as something comes closer to surfacing. If the past few years were about breaking down after losing Brent and breaking out of my old life in Alaska, then this year feels like my breakthrough year.

So often this past year I've felt like I've been diligently working behind the scenes. Building a new business, doing deep inner soul work, learning about the nature of the universe through the process of living, observing, and examination. Recalibrating and coming to a deeper space of alignment within myself.

It's been hard work, without a lot of recognition or validation *(most inner work is like that, which is why it's inner work and the invisible process of the soul)*. But now I feel on the cusp, like my invisible process of soul is about to become more visible through my words and the work I'm trying to bring into the world.

I feel ready. I'd like to know what the next chapter holds.

I've often felt a sense of fatigue this past year. I've been following my invisible, intuitive path with many twists and turns, and I keep faithfully showing up. Trusting my process of soul. Trusting I'm unfolding as I should. Trusting the calling I feel inside without any blueprint of what it will look like.

That's where the fatigue comes in: no blueprint, not a lot of structure, not a lot of external validation. Just me going inwards, trusting spirit, and approaching each day with creative intent and listening to my inclinations and intuitions on what I need to create that day, without any guarantees that *if I build it, they will come.*

Self-doubt and insecurity can be fierce beasts. I've had to root a lot out in this process. Get past my own blocks: Will anyone take my online courses? Will people see the value in my individual services and the skill set I bring to the table with my psychological and intuitive background? Will my books ever sell more than a couple handfuls of copies?

Will I be able to make my living as a creative? Will I ever get more than 3 views when I post a YouTube video, whose healing content took me time and energy to craft? Will I always feel lost in the shuffle and overlooked professionally? Will my work ever land and start sticking with the people I'm meant to connect, serve, and be in community with?

I believe the answers to these questions are a resounding, yes. It's taken me a lot of deep inner work to build a sense of confidence and assuredness, but that's part of soul work and rooting out doubts. Those doubts have made me examine, on an even deeper level, what I believe about this universe and my relationship with spirit.

I believe I've been given my creative dreams and visions for a purpose.

Much of my time in Kauai has been a practice in radical self-belief. In knowing that numbers, followers, book sales, and external signs of "success" don't necessarily constitute success or value. In understanding: while I haven't found a bigger sense of community and tribe so far, it doesn't mean I won't.

I've had to learn to show up for myself in bigger ways over here. To show up for my dreams, to seed them and protect their seeds. To fight for them and for my right to live a life of joy and creativity.

Those are my lessons of the latter half of 2018: just keep showing up.

So, I have, and a lot of creativity and growth has come from that. Now I feel poised for the next level. For speaking, teaching, and engaging with others in bigger ways. I've written my symphony, now my desire is to connect with the people who value my music.

That music is the fire within me. Humming, strumming, thrumming, drumming, ready to be let out.

I did an oracle reading for 2019 the other day. I've been using my meditation time to take inventory, close out 2018, and set my vision for what I'd like to create in 2019. The last card in the reading was "Volcano" and the words that went with the card said:

"It's been building for a while now, and you are ready to burst out with a bang! They better watch out for you sweetheart because you are about to bring the fire." I'm ready. I'm a spark waiting to blaze and bring the fire, bring the music, bring the symphony to life.

Bring myself out into this world in bigger ways.

46

SERENGETI DREAMS

A new day dawns
in jungle speak —
which sings to
the heart of my
Serengeti dreams.

Windy greens
and tree soul beats —
drumming the
waves of
emerald weaves.

They tell me to
embrace possibility —
the pages of blank
for what can and
will be...
to release
rigidity,
timelines,
and histories,
— which don't serve
the growth of my
soul's forest deep.

To take
each moment as it
crystalizes
and frees —
*create the life
I hope I'll be.*

47

Rose Gardens in the Stars

W hatever it is that you're dreaming about — dream bigger. Don't waste time thinking about how it's going to happen or if it's possible or how you will get there — just start by dreaming. Start by allowing yourself to imagine something beyond what you have previously imagined. Start with the seed of a rose and imagine planting an entire garden.

Imagine a rose garden blooming in the stars.

Allow your mind to expand and grow: the only way to free ourselves from limitations and invite MORE into our lives is to keep pushing through our previous limitations. Be open and stay curious, feed your heart with what tastes good to your heart. Remember leaps of faith start with pointing our internal compass towards our wishes, hopes, and dreams.

We take flight by making one small step after another as we keep building momentum in our dream's direction.

Our lives will only be as big as our dreams allow. That must begin inside — within our mind and our heart and our spirit — before the universe can respond to our intent, will, energy, and desire and help bring opportunities into our path to help us build and create our dreams.

This is what co-creativity is all about: *a continuous dance with the cosmos as we dream big and keep putting ourselves and our dreams out there, then create with the ingredient's life brings us.* We become bigger through each act of dream as we keep growing our gardens towards the stars.

48

TANGLED

*J*anuary is always a strange month for me. There's a sense of void and blankness that comes with the dawn of a new year. A sense of emptiness following the bustle of the holiday season.

But mostly, there's a sense of twisted feelings. A complex web of emotions that originates from losing Brent in January 2016. Like gnarled roots, my feelings tether me to the earth in deeper ways, yet their knots delineate the messiness of my grief journey and the tangled ways we find grace in grief.

Some days I still can't believe this is my life, even as I've had three years to live the loss and process the knowledge: *this is how our sibling story played out — one life interrupted and my life permanently changed.*

The hardest part of grief is often not the losing. It is living day in and day out with the losing, while life spins on around you. Carrying the burden of grief inside of you. Carting around the invisible scars left by the wound of loss. You feel like you're bleeding out internally, and there is no way to staunch the flow.

Initially, it took me about six months before I finally had a sense the flow was gradually easing.

During that time, I passed through many lands in Griefdom. *The Deep Sea of Sorrow. The Rage Stage. The Barren Wasteland. The Me That Will Never Be.* The eye of an intense, disorienting, emotional storm I named *Chaos and Love.*

I unraveled. I dissolved. I struggled. I crawled.

I put on my front person, showed up at my psychological practice, and kept going the best I knew how. Sometimes it helped to shift gears and focus on others. Here was one area of my life that still felt the same when everything inside of me felt different.

In my alone time, I wrote my heart out and incubated. People probably felt like I'd ghosted them, but what they didn't know is I was a ghost in my own life, stuck between worlds. Trying to build a bridge between life and death, so I could fully understand the nature of dying.

What people didn't know is that some part of me died too when I lost Brent, and I needed to come to terms with myself.

Come to terms with death. Come to terms with life. Come to terms that BethAnne and Brent's timeline on earth ended when he was 39. Come to terms with a burgeoning sense of Brent's spiritual presence as I worked on integrating the idea he still existed, just in different form.

It is the nature of the introvert-intuitive soul to go inward, feel, and sense when the heart is being cracked open. I burrowed inwards. I mined my feelings and my experience of self, searching for truth and understanding.

In the three years since Brent has passed, I've come to see that some part of myself will never fully understand his loss, even as other parts have made peace and found acceptance. Some things in life come to pass in ways that are messy, imperfect, and irresolute. I've learned in a visceral way that life's irresolution is often opportunity for creative evolution.

I had to stretch out and grow beyond my previous version of self to start my healing process. After my initial grief contraction, I needed to learn to stand and expand. Reach for higher perspective and develop a keen gaze for finding the light hiding in life's breaks.

I found deeper compassion, mercy for the difficult process of being human, and a profound sense of gratitude for my life. Inner strength was waiting for me to recognize my own strength and claim it, because after a time I realized I was doing the impossible — carrying the loss, carrying Brent, carrying my burden of grief.

I became a stronger, braver woman in my process, and I realized everything about my grief was born out of love, because grief and love are two sides of the same coin: *we grieve because we have loved and will always love.*

The love that unraveled me became the same love that helped me begin to knit my seams back together. I restitched myself with greater authenticity, a heart filled with hard earned wisdom, and the transcendent effects of my grief odyssey. I came to see I had poured myself out when I lost Brent, and in that process, something more soulful and spirit-filled poured into my hollow bones, filling me with bright knowledge.

It was in this grace space that I decided to radically change my life. I did by leaving Alaska and moving to Kauai a year later. That transition is another journey of loving, losing, destruction, and reconstruction, and Brent is tangled up in all of it.

It strikes me so often I wouldn't be here, living my leap of faith on this island, if not for Brent. I wouldn't have become who I've become — a grief author, teacher, and sacred space holder for grievers — if not for Brent. His loss became part of the bedrock I planted my roots in, and yet it is very much my choice to hold space for grief, as I have come to see this as holy work.

I honor Brent when I hold space. I honor myself. I honor Life. I honor Spirit. I honor the invisible soul calling that keeps pulling me forwards in my life.

There hasn't been a day that's gone by since January 18, 2016, when I haven't thought about Brent.

Some days it's a lingering missing and loss of presence. Some days it's an awareness of the whole, a deeper reflection of all that's transpired since my loss. Some days it's wonder at Life's strange mysteries and a vow to keep living well by embracing my moments.

Some days it's all of that and more:

A rainbow of colors descends upon my wise-oak bark and gnarled roots. I am anchored to the grace of the earth, even as I have visions and glimpses of what lays beyond those colors. I can feel my human and my divine meeting somewhere in-between.

Brent is always there in the in-between.

He wraps his scarlet soul-scarf around my mahogany branches, and we wave in the wind together, as the rest of the world fades away. We whisper, him and I, of days gone by, who we've become, and all that's come to pass.

In those moments we are one, and I see the illusion for what it is, and I know that all that matters most was and is the love.

49

GRIEF, THE GREAT EQUALIZER

*W*ater is an element that cleanses everybody. It strips away the dirt and the grit — it purifies and renews.

Grief has the power to do that too. It's supposed to unravel, it's supposed to undo — that's the chaos of it — like a storm hitting our lands. Grief is designed to deconstruct our finite ego and take us into our infinite soul. It holds the power to potentially purify through its wisdom, because grief's wisdom is the wisdom of love.

Love, even disguised as grief, is always the great equalizer. Cutting through all layers, barriers, and boundaries. Asking us to peel away our ideals, so we can travel closer to the soul of what is most real.

50

THE CONSTANT CONNECTOR

I magine how a mountain with all its terrain can be so expansive and vast, yet it is all the same mountain.

The bottom of the mountain is in a different space than the top of the mountain, yet they are still related and connected. The tree at the base of the hill is in a different place than the tree at the top, yet they still belong to the same hill.

Think of all the flowers, birds, plants, animals, and pines belonging to the land. They may give the illusion of being separate elements, yet they are all interconnected and part of the mountain's whole.

Imagine how the earth is so wonderfully big and complex.

The Arctic ice and Sahara sands are nowhere close to one another, and yet they are still part of the same earth. From the vastness of the ocean to the smallness of a pond, water is still water and is also part of the same earth.

The Great Barrier Reef and the majesty of Mount Denali do not need to be side by side to belong to the same earth. The natural world knows it's all connected, because it is connected by the core of the same earth.

Maybe this principal is a metaphor for how we connect with those we've loved and lost.

We can't see them or touch them. They feel like they've left us and are gone. But if Love is eternal and we come from Love, then Love becomes the core that keeps us connected.

We don't have to be physically side by side to be spiritually side by side. We don't have to be on the same mountain in the physical plane to be able to meet on Love's mountain in the spiritual plane. We just have to free ourselves from the illusion of separation and focus on the love we have for our loved ones.

We can reach them through our hearts, we can feel them through our hearts, we can speak to them through our hearts, and we can hear them in our hearts, because LOVE is the constant connector.

51

Heaven's Doves

There is a gentleness
to the yellow flower
which belies its ability
to bloom
magnificently —
regardless of any
eyes who may see.

The pine leaves
weave on the breeze
with careless regard
for scrutiny —
pleasure is their
treasure-seek,
existing in delight for
no reason 'cept being.

A drop of water
can make the ocean greater,
even as the ocean
engulfs the drop,
and grief and love
can fly side by side,
strings of pearls
on heaven's doves.

I sense you arrive
on a silver sky
a voice from beyond
on the day you crossed sides —

"Don't try so hard to always do
or worry when you'll be seen —
Little Sister, I want you to be happy.
it is enough to exist, to joy, to be."

52

ANNIVERSARY

Dear Brent,
(AKA Big Brother, Brent the Gray and Brother Skywalker)

It's been a long day without you my friend, and today's the day we try and make it to the Super Bowl again. I've got your lucky jersey on, so here's hoping.

This week marked three years since you've been gone, and there's so much I want to tell you, though I believe you already know. You're the reason I'm wearing Gronk '87 and care about football in the first place.

You've become so much a part of me since you've been gone, sometimes I'm not sure where my grief-love ends and I begin… then again that sort of doesn't matter, since life is composed of endless cycles anyways. All I can do is try and be like the moon and embrace all my faces.

For the record, I don't believe you care too much about who wins games these days. I get the strong sense you've expanded WAY beyond that in ways I can't fully comprehend. But I absolutely believe you care about our family's well-being, so I know you'll be watching today and wishing us joy.

Win or lose, it's all good, we got our underdog 28–3, Disney ending comeback in 2017…. but I'd love to make it to the bowl one more time, while the team still looks close to how you'd remember them. *You see, change often aches Big Brother, there is comfort in familiarity, and sometimes part of me wants to slow it down for a bit and stop life's constant revolutions.*

But here we are — me Here, and you There — and you're loved and missed even as life keeps moving forward. I watched Dad and Mom celebrate their 50th without you this past year, and though I know you can still see us, I wish you were here in person to see who our family has become. I think you'd be proud.

We love you Brent. We honored you in our own ways this week. And whatever happens today, I'll see you in the sky afterwards, somewhere between the eclipse and the full moon. Where the boundaries are blurred, things are softer, and grace becomes the golden medium filling this space.

Love,
BethAnne
(AKA Little Sister, Sister Leia and Meriadoc Brandybuck)

53

Year of The Pig

I read somewhere that January would be a slower month, as if we were all moving underwater, and I felt that molasses-type feel last month.

I've had a slight sense of disconnect and slowing, as if I'm not quite seeing the bigger picture — my bigger picture — and there's a forced patience towards my process, since I've been impatient to see my bigger picture from the moment I arrived on Kauai.

This is not my first forced patience. I'm well-practiced at this point in making myself slow down, turn inwards, and intuitively listen to what step I need to take that day. Do this each day and the bigger "next step" eventually unveils itself.

This slowing is an odd juxtaposition compared to the sense of active fire energy I felt as we transitioned into 2019. I'm hungry for something this year — growth, greater clarity, an illuminated step on my professional and spiritual path, a bigger glimpse of how my picture fits into Spirit's bigger picture.

Since it's after midnight as I write this, and I'm midnight snackish hungry, a food metaphor comes to mind: I feel as if I've been invited to dinner, and I'm anticipating this really gorgeous feast (I do so love food). Yet upon arrival, I'm told the table isn't quite ready, so it's going to take longer than planned, then I'm ushered into a side waiting room and given a small plate of cheese and crackers to tide me over.

Cheese and crackers are pleasing, but it's nowhere near enough to satisfy the hunger inside of me.

It's a strange thing to live with big dreams. I've made great strides towards them, and yet I find an ongoing tension between the bigger picture and the day to day. Focus too much on the bigger picture, and I lose the joy contained in each day. Focus too much on the day to day, and I lose my bigger picture of all the things I wish to create, dream, and carry out.

I've tried to settle on an in-between where each week I line out my goals and intentions, then adjust accordingly as the week spins out. There is a relaxed, loose sense to it, while still maintaining a framework for spontaneous possibility.

It's a grounded approach, and I'm reminded that we just entered the Year of the Pig on the lunar new year calendar. The element is earth, which is good for grounding energy. And it's supposed to be a good year for luck.

I'm smiling as I write these words. Pigs in Kauai are prolific and obnoxious. Living up by the jungle it's not uncommon to wake up to find 10–20 in our back yard, digging up and rooting in the soil, and tearing up the lawn. Our dog Frodo hates them and goes into hyper-alert-Orc-hunting mode, while he runs around the house, barking his head off. *We've lost a lot of sleep, because of the pigs.*

I'm smiling again as a deeper memory of a pig tugs at the recesses of my mind.

The day I moved out of my office on June 29, 2017, is one of the most surreal days of my life. After over 10 years in that building, I sat in my therapist chair, staring out the window, watching the movers cart all the big furniture away. Everything else has already been donated, tossed, or relocated. I only have a small bag of items I'm taking with me, which feels like a clean break.

The movers remove my therapist chair last. It seems poetic. Alone in my empty office, I close the door and say a final goodbye, while I let the strange, twisted feels of closing this particular chapter pour through me like the rain outside. Then I notice a tiny object laying on the floor in an otherwise barren space: a little black and white pig with an adorable snout.

It had been a part of my miniature collection, which hung on my wall for all those years. I'd donated the collection weeks earlier, but somehow this pig didn't make it to donation. Instead, there it lay on the floor of my empty office like a tiny talisman. I look up the symbolism of the pig and see pigs represent prosperity, good luck, and good fortune. I decide this is an auspicious omen of good things to come.

My tiny porcelain pig made it to the island with me, where it rests in a small jar I keep on the bottom of my nightstand, also containing a penny, white feather, and a scrap of paper, which says "for luck."

I almost forgot about my lucky pig, and as I sit here writing these words, I'm reassured by the memory of the constant synchronicities and little moments of magic in our lives. They remind us we are constantly guided and there IS a bigger picture. Everything is working together in its own divine, chaotic, splendor to create the bigger whole.

We're each umbrella-ed under the bigger whole. As such, I remind myself even in this strange foggy feeling state, I'm right where I need to be.

Planting my feet on the solid ground of Kauai. Still listening. Taking one step after the other, as I slowly move towards my dreams. Reminding myself *receptivity and being* are equally important to *decision and action.*

I can have spirit-inspired ambition and heart-based dreams, and trust those inner ingredients will keep alchemizing and re-alchemizing until they create whatever mixture is required for my own greater good. I remember my water wisdom of last summer and early fall: *Flow with grace and ease. Take small tangible steps. Be fluid. Let life be fluid. Lean into the energy. Invite Spirit into the mix. Trust that it will take me where it may.*

Remember small steps add up to bigger steps.

For now, small steps it is as I reformulate and let what will be form. In the meantime, I'll take my wisdom from pig spirit and remember abundance, opportunity, and good fortune await. We don't have to see them to believe they are there, we just have to trust and stay open.

54

Tree Harmonies

They can reach
on a beach —
up to the sky
in wayward symphony.

Or grow
in a grove
where their soul
is so old, they're
fast friends with
the ancient sages
of stones.

Or seed
in the green
— spruce shoots
and saplings,
whose spurts
are yet to be
seen.

But field
forest or sea,
young, old or
in-between
a tree is still
a tree —

A teacher of
oneness and connectivity.

Helping us
remember our
peace is found
in harmony
— when we
learn to be.

55

THE NATURE OF YOU

*W*e can be very impatient in our change process. We judge a bad day, a bad month, a bad season as evidence we are not changing quickly enough, or we have wasted time and gone backwards. Then in our self-judgment we feel even further away from the place we are trying to get to.

Isn't it fortunate then when we get into the shame spaces inside of ourselves, where the mind says "you're not doing it quickly enough and you will never get there;" we have magnificent teachers in nature who teach us the exact opposite?

Nature teaches us we can't actually stop change from happening. We can't stop a season or force a season. Nature teaches us change often happens on its own accord. Just like the trees, flowers, moon and sun, and natural rhythms of life: we too are in a constant state of transformation within our own cycle and rhythm of self.

If you are seeking change and trying to get somewhere, but don't feel like you are doing it fast enough — rest easy. All things truly do happen in their own time. Including you.

If you are seeking change yet feel stuck and like you're not taking the right steps to make things different — rest easy. Just because you can't see the seeds being planted doesn't mean they won't bloom and bud in time, helping you find your momentum.

If you don't know where you're at with any of it — rest easy. A tree cannot help but be a tree, and a flower cannot help but be a flower. A cloud will naturally embody the nature of a cloud, and a stone cannot help but embody the energy of being a stone.

So, if you just relax around all of it and allow yourself patience with your own growth and truth, you will find that so as with nature, you cannot help but embody the nature of you.

56

The Signature of Hope

*H*ope makes all the difference in regard to the lens with which we view the world.

The jungle is cloudy with unshed rain as I write these words. The roosters are strumming and humming outside my window, and lavender tea cools in my favorite blue mug while I meditate upon my history with hope.

I'm not quite sure when or why it happened, but I found myself penning the words, "In hope," on my writer's page sometime in the new year. The words stuck and have become my signature sign off. I used to sign "in love" or "in peace," both very good things as well, but there is something about the essence of hope, which speaks towards reaching and growing in a direction of optimism and wellness.

When I was younger, hope was something connected to the desire for a specific outcome. Hope came with a large dose of expectations, which inevitably created a roller coaster effect. Life hopefully swung up when my expectations were met and hopelessly dropped down when they weren't.

It was during the period of 2011–2014 that my relationship with hope got its most significant overhaul. This is the post-divorce window in my life, and I was finding my real self for the first time. As a byproduct, I did a lot of deep soul searching and internal work.

At the time, life came with some serrated edges, which scraped against my vulnerable heart. It was an extremely human space of learning and becoming.

I learned how to cultivate inner peace, even if life isn't peaceful. I learned to find joy for the little things, so my happiness is less contingent on circumstances and more contingent on paying attention to beauty. Many painful experiences happened in that time, but I found the silver lining of pain is the opportunity to grow, gain higher perspective, and find transformative ways of being.

I often refer to those years as "the growing up years," where I crammed much wisdom and knowledge into a condensed space. My mentor once told me it was like I had lived 10 years in a few, and as the one who experienced those years and has witnessed my own change, I have to agree.

I learned in that time that having a steady sense of hope isn't found in the specific outcome of a situation, but hope is always found when we let our mind's eye take in the whole and believe that the creative mysteries are taking us in a direction of growth.

When we lost Brent in 2016, hope was greatly challenged. There is nothing like death to take you to the core of who you are and put under the microscope what you believe about life, love, and the workings of the universe.

The nature of grief is disarray, and as I wandered through the chaos, I had to learn how to reassemble myself into something more than I was before. Grief is at times a hopeless place, and when the very worst of it had passed and I was able to stand up, I had to fight to reclaim the good.

I fought for joy. I fought for gratitude. I fought for hope. I fought for bigger perspective of the whole, and I learned the lessons of my growing up years all over again in bigger, more integrated ways.

I learned to find beauty, even when the mudslides of life pool in messy masses around your feet and threaten to take you under. I learned to dig down and in, instead of wallow in the why, and find the diamonds that form under duress. I learned to reach high and wide and bring starlight into deep midnight, so I always had something to set my compass by.

Hope became the signature penned upon my heart, which held me steady and reminded me that even when life tips over, the innate intelligence and love of the universe will be there to help us absorb the tip and find the gifts in falling sideways.

I think it is human nature to hope for better things, but the shift between my younger-self and my now-self is an openness to what those better things are.

Maybe better things don't have to look a certain way but are found on a simple Sunday as you sip your coffee and stare out at the jungle in wonder and gratitude, noticing the way the malachite green brushes against dove sky.

Maybe better things are found every time we choose resilience over despair, stepping more fully into our infinite selves by believing in the invisible and inexorable heartbeat of love that surrounds and infuses this place.

Maybe better things are a refusal to give up hope, even when the world feels hopeless, because we know the stars are still guiding and the sun will still rise, and as long as there's a rise there is hope.

Maybe better things are found in unnoticed places, but the moment we take the time to notice them we realize how rich life is with betterment.

I made it through last month like a marathon and a sprint: slow and steady mixed with short bursts and gasps. January is not the easiest month for me. Brent's been gone three years now.

Perhaps three years is the beginning of a bigger bird's eye view that will keep growing in time, as I keep gaining deeper insight and awareness over who I've become in my loss and how grief has changed me. Grief threw me into a stormy sea of dissolution and disarray, and as my former self dissolved, I learned to swim through the tempest and float.

In that place, I searched for hope and found, though invisible, if you insist on believing in its existence —

Hope is only a signature away.

57

THE WHOLE ROSE

*T*hrough grappling we find growth. We find insights, we give ourselves permission not to know and stay open to finding out. We find the diamonds in the mud and figure out how to work around a rose's thorns and see the beauty of the rose's whole. *We show up for ourselves when we work through our thorns and come to see the beauty in the whole of our being.*

When we do that, we make space for the whole of our experience, so we are not afraid to show up, listen, learn, and evolve our heart wisdom.

58

Ship of Fools

*I*t is a blustery gray day on the island. March comes with cool breezes, silver skies, and a bevy of piglets taking over the grounds round our house.

One night, before sunset, the cat and I sat watching them run across the yard. A cluster of squeals and confusion, like a swine clown car unloosed. The Grateful Dead's *Ship of Fools* happens to be playing in the background, and by the lofty look of disdain on the cat's face, I can tell she thinks the song apropos.

The piggy's chaotic meanderings are the epitome of being on a ship of fools; messy and directionless, they scamper about in our yard to and fro, not quite sure of what direction they are going.

I understand this lost feeling, because I feel like I'm on the ship of fools as well right now. This winter has brought a strong sense of stopping and going, without a lot of momentum being gained, even as I can see that movement IS happening.

I'm in an in-between space, wondering which way to sail, the same old directionless feeling resurfacing, as I wonder about my way forward on this island and in my greater service. I'm only on year two of my Kauai journey and I already have senioritis, wishing I had graduated through my transition and moved into a more anchored, secure place.

My husband is on the ship too having the same stop and go as myself. After laboring away to pass his real estate board exams, he had to wait months before the board approved him. Due to an incident long in his past, we ended up on Oahu last Friday where he spoke to the board. Hopeful we'd know something that day, we felt spent when they told him to call on Monday for their decision.

We wandered around Waikiki the rest of the day in a haze feeling like country mice in the big city as we talked about how difficult things have been for us on Kauai. This is a hard island to get a good-paying job on. The stress of the board's decision weighs

113

heavy. So does the knowledge we are on this island because of me, and better opportunity for him could be found elsewhere.

It is a long weekend. Even the dog feels the stress, gets jungle fever, and runs off on our favorite mountain while he and I hiked. After 45 minutes of panic, prayer, tears, and desperation, I climb down a jungle ravine and cry in relief when I found his filthy, foolish self. We emerge from the trail, two mud covered yetis, and I go home and collapse from the compounded stress.

We receive a *yes* from the board come Monday. My parents treat us to celebratory dinner. By Tuesday, I feel the stress-fatigue creep and settle into my body, brought on by the ongoing questions of who we're becoming on this island and how we'll financially make ends meet.

The *yes* is a ray of hope. A license doesn't equate a living right away. But it's a start. As I said earlier, movement IS happening. But even the movement in our professional lives seems to be on island time, and nothing has coalesced with quick ease.

The pigs, my husband, and I have a couple other passengers on our ship of fools. The dog is traveling with us, busy barking and obsessing over the pigs, while the cat sits port side, presiding over all, while managing to look simultaneously contemptuous and all-knowing. She seems to know something we don't about the strange turnings, meanderings, and rhythms of life.

I have to remind myself being a fool isn't necessarily a bad thing. In the tarot deck, the first card is The Fool. It's an optimistic card. Being The Fool represents new beginnings, taking leaps of faith, wandering outside the lines, and following the purity of our heart's dreams with wide-eyed innocence. *The Fool knows we will never actualize a dream if we don't take that first step into the unknown.*

I've been The Fool a lot on this island. I'm not quite so wide-eyed innocent now, but I am wandering, following the purity of my heart's intent, and staying open to how my leap of faith unfolds. I did this to myself. I chose to leap, and I'm fully aware I purposefully lost myself by choosing to follow soul's call.

"New tide, surprise, my world is changing. Within this frame an ocean swells behind the smile, I know it well. Beneath a lover's moon, I'm waiting. I am the pilot of the storm, adrift in pleasure

I may drown. I built this ship it is my making... Crazy on a ship of fools."

It is my making. I did build this ship, and I am crazy on a ship of fools.

Like I said earlier, maybe that's not such a bad thing. Maybe we all sail the ship of fools from time to time in our lives, and it's just a rite of passage of being human. We wander outside the lines, so we can learn to chart a new course. We lose ourselves to find ourselves. We try to find ways to anchor in life's storms, ride them out, and see what breaks on new dawn.

Maybe we all need a lesson from the pigs on how to weather life's change and keep ourselves anchored to the ground:

It's okay to be messy. Return to the earth when you need centering. Don't take yourself so seriously you fear looking foolish and lost, for it is only churning through life's mud our deepest treasures are forged and found.

59

Winds of Change

*I*t's funny how goodness often comes with a side of chaos.

As if the universe works in waves and flows, where new individual energy rides the crest of and arrives on a bigger tide of collective energy. You want to celebrate and revel in the beauty of the moment, yet the winds of change are swirling all around you (literally) and instead of celebrating, you're dealing with a power outage, fallen trees, and a rapidly thawing refrigerator.

This is a beautiful illustration of my time on Kauai, as I've often found that on this island good things happen, but they can tumble in sideways, swept around by the elements and the power of this tiny isle of land, which packs a big punch.

I received news this weekend that I am going to be a speaker in April at a professional psychological conference.

I got the news in the middle of a windstorm; the microcosm-flurry of excitement inside of me matching and reflecting the macrocosm of the bigger flurry of excitement outside. With the power out, no internet, and wind howling around, cocooning in bed seemed like a solid choice, and I lay there for a while and cried.

Tears of joy. Tears of overwhelm. Tears of witness for the journey I've taken to get to this point: this is my first time speaking at this big of an event. I totally believe in myself even as I feel the rush of unknown anticipation that occurs when we step into uncharted territory and don't know what we'll find.

It's hard to keep stoking the embers of a dream when you don't have tangible results of your dream. I have fire within me I've been trying to release but finding the spaces that value my light and need my spark has been a process of creative reinvention and steep learning curves. Part of the process has been finding out the journey of starting over at mid-life on an island is not always the easiest, nor what I expected.

Kauai has big energy; she will shake you up and rearrange you.

I wasn't expecting the lightning bolts of transformation which have transpired here. There have been many times where I've struggled to move in the direction of my dreams when they haven't coalesced, and I've been forced to keep the faith in my soul calling and invisible pull of my heart.

I've also learned soul callings don't mean everything lines up right away. They just mean, if you're following your intuitive guidance you will absolutely keep moving in the right direction, even if you feel like you're moving in circles and waves.

Like the wind outside making everything swirl and whirl in celestine visions of blue-gray and pewter-breath; you can't see where it's coming from, but its force is undeniable. So, it is with the mysteries: an invisible but undeniable force. When we answer the call of our soul, we are answering this force, placing ourselves in its hands and saying, "I trust, I trust, I trust."

Even when I can't see the way.

I do feel the way, however.

I feel the rightness and resonance to my choices, even if I don't know the bigger picture I'm creating. I feel the vibration and vibrancy for my bigger visions of speaking, teaching, and working with a global reach. I feel the inspiration and anticipation that comes from following a dream and being a participant and observer of how it unfolds.

I've begun to see the past couple years were years for living the questions, and this year will be a year finding answers. Maybe not all the answers, but it's a start. I write these words with gratitude in my heart, because I've been seeding and kindling my dreams for so long and waiting for something to land and stick.

This speaking opportunity is a stick.

Even the winds rattling the windows can't blow it away or make me change momentum, so I'll just try and blow with them for a while and find movement in this new direction. Trusting I'm absolutely on the path and every step I've taken was needed to get me to where I am today.

It's not always easy to keep the faith when we can't see the evidence or results (which is precisely what faith is all about — keeping vision in the absence of sight). But it will always be worth it, because we can always trust our soul.

Even though there will be days where you feel lost as you wander the wild unknown, tumbling about like a tumbleweed in the wind while you learn to surrender over and over. There are also days where that congratulatory email will finally come —

And you know you were headed in the right direction all along, as you prepare to reach, then reach some more, and pull yourself up to the next level.

60

ASILOMAR COAST

*F*ar from home and so ready to become more. I'm nervous. Excited. Brimming with bearing witness to the journey which traveled me here.

The coast quickly becomes my friend. Turquoise waters anchor. Wind whips with unfamiliar chills, but the warmth of golden flowers and tangy orange punches of bloom mixes with bunnies, reminding me: *I always belong in nature. No matter where.*

Running is my friend in times like this, and I find myself working through myself as steady footfalls mix with crashes of waves.

How did I get here? Ready to speak. Ready to share. Ready to become more than where I've been.

Some days it seems like Brent is still alive, and it's all been a dream. Most days I know the dream is the illusion of loss. Today I hear Brent's voice through the sky as one of my Brent Songs plays on my headphones at 11:11.

Three dogs running on the beach all happily descend on me at that moment, and I laugh with joy, as if the spirit world sent ambassadors to remind me of their presence.

The sky opens up then, while the sun falls down in crystal rays. I don't want to leave this magical time with Brent, for I sense he's right there with me.

The tears come in waves, along with the waves of the sea; we wander so far from home only to find ourselves again. Find the space inside of ourselves, which anchors us and ripples with resonance and belonging.

Inviting us to return to the love within and remember *love is the master weaver who keeps us always connected.*

61

THE CONTRARIAN

Sometimes life will
teach it to us upside down:
from butterfly to cocoon
from tomb to womb.

Nautilus unspiraling
westward sunrise rising
clockwise counter timing
walking backwards in a room.

Where Jupiter's retrograde
becomes heart's renegade
to learn new truths in contrary ways —
composing a symphony off-tune.

*(To break us down
and wake us out
and shake our former views)*

My heart unloves
in beats and shades
becoming brighter with each moon:

To relearn love in greater ways —
Loving backward in the room.

62

Ecosystem

*W*hat if when things go wrong, they are still going right? What if the things we like least about ourselves have the most to teach us? What if the pieces of ourselves we think we are missing are actually inside us all along, slowly coming up and crystallizing so we can realize them?

What if our soul knows exactly what it's doing, and it's just interfacing with this world in a way that feels topsy-turvy, because we don't always understand its methods?

What if we turn our self-hierarchies upside down and learn to see the value and wisdom from whatever we deem as *on the bottom?* What if we trade our hierarchies for circles, where everything has a place in the whole of our eco-system?

What if vulnerability becomes our fiercest strength and owning "I don't know" is exactly what we need to find our knowing?

What if we start where we are at each day, believe we're enough, and know whatever aspects of self that emerge have purpose and contribution to our greater whole?

What if our personal evolution becomes a revolution of radical acceptance and love: *Knowing each of us will be whoever we are meant to be — we don't have to try so hard.* Knowing we will fulfill whatever purpose we are called to fulfill — the universe is ripe and abundant and will not withhold all the good and beautiful things promised to each.

Knowing we ARE embodying our soul path through the simple act of living — we don't have to be anyone or anything special, we just have to be ourselves. When we're doing this (even if we don't quite know who or what or where we are at times), we cannot lose our way.

We can rest in the knowledge that all of it — all the twists, turns, detours, and losing then finding ourselves — is just a part of our path. And I believe each of us is already walking the path beautifully, my brave, fellow souls.

63

RECKONING

S ometimes, it does not go the way you play it in your head. I came. I spoke. I learned.

My first speaking engagement left me mixed. In part, because my supremely prepared, perfectionist, idealistic nature encountered a different set up than what I'd expected. I was rapidly readjusting expectations while I was speaking and simultaneously realizing I was not going to deliver a home run speech to a captive audience.

I did, however, do my best to keep going, and say what I came to say to a room that was slightly chaotic. People were coming and going, a few were completely checked out because they were there to hear the person going after me, and I couldn't have been paired with two more diverse presenters. Our topics were not compatible, and I could feel the weight of disappointment sink into my stomach when I finished, settled down into my seat and tried, to attend to my fellow colleague's talks.

Life, eh?

I had a good cry at the beach when it was all done. I've been carrying so much for so long ever since I lost Brent, following this invisible heart path, doing the brave scary things. As much as I speak about releasing expectations of outcome, I realized I had attached an expectation to the conference and what might blossom from there.

I so badly want to find the community and people I connect with who want to hear my message.

This wasn't quite it.

I had to reach for higher perspective and remind myself just because my talk didn't go exactly as I'd desired, it didn't mean the weekend didn't unfold according to what my soul needed.

The location itself was by the ocean, and the coastal views and Californian wildflowers mixed with the scent of juniper and pine was a gift. I saw deer several mornings on the campus I was staying, and truly appreciated the majestic beauty of wild spaces. The salt-tang of the ocean breeze inspired my poet's heart with words, images, and creative musings.

I felt Brent close by often and kept receiving 11:11's, 2:22's, and 4:44's along with other signs and symbols, which made me feel held and endeared by spirit.

A dear friend from Alaska happened to be in Pacific Grove, a stone's throw away, at the time of the conference. She showed up with encouragement, pride, friendship, and made me feel like a million bucks. I held onto her presence as the silver lining of my talk.

I made a couple cosmic connections; individuals I kept intersecting with at random intervals and having the most delightful conversations. Whether they turn out to be friends, allies, or just a momentary connection to remind me I'm not alone in the universe or my healing path — that warmed my heart too.

Magic IS happening, but it's not always in the ways we expect.

I believe that is my biggest take home. The realization I had an idea of "what and how" in my mind, which did not come to fruition. Yet that doesn't mean the cosmos' *How* wasn't exactly meant to be.

I keep learning as I walk this path of trust with spirit: it often doesn't look the way you think it will, and I need to learn to make peace with that. This is not an easy task, yet as much as I burn with a desire for something bigger, I still can't quite define, I keep coming back to the moment of now and balancing desire with contentment.

A year ago, I was having an epiphany that I wanted to be much further along on the journey than I found myself my first year in Kauai. Now it's a year later, and I AM further along, and yet I still want to be even further. I find myself circling back to last year's lessons as I remember the importance of simply being present and finding joy in the NOW.

Perhaps a year from now, I'll find myself in the same boat. Further along than now, yet still restless for more. Some of that is just part of who I am. With my Gemini Jupiter in my 9th house of publication and my Leo Sun in my 10th house of career — expansion of wisdom, knowledge, communication and career ambition are in my personality's constellation.

Yet my Sagittarius Moon in 3rd says: "Be curious now, find joy now, be happy now, carpe diem and do not waste this day."

I'm trying to grab onto that right now.

Readjust. Reorient. Release expectation. Receive where I'm at. Strive to find the joy. Quiet the disquiet in my restless heart who craves answers and movement. Stick with myself and my Kauai journey and trust.

Trust the magic.

Even in the face of all that lays unseen.

64

Bluebird Jams & Exhortations on Living

es, dear humans, yes. Just be in the full of your experience, let it be what it is, and learn to find the music in every note.

That is how you find the joy in the day.

Be present. Listen. Make art. Write. Breathe your being into your creativity so you're fully present in your words.

Others can wait. Others will have to wait. You can't always be about the other and also be about you.

Take this grace space of now and find joy and pleasure. Make peace with where you're at and the ongoing nebula that is the future. Go find a mountain and sit on top of it. Be romanced by the earth and romance it straight back.

Let your notes be a jam, or the Blues, or a symphony, or a pop song, or a single key off-beat and off-tune.

It doesn't matter, dear soul, as long as it's the truest reflection of you and your truth.

65

I Wonder, and I Wander

*T*he light gets brighter and hotter as April unwinds into May and I wander through the springtime, feeling like I've lost my way.

I returned to the island deflated after I spoke. I believed I would realize my next step in California. I did not. I am still unclear, and I don't have a strong sense of what's next in my intuitive world or in the external world.

I'm working on a new poetry book, which feels optimistic, but all else feels fearfully quiet on the work front. The courses I worked so hard to craft are not selling. My clients are dwindling. I know I'm meant to speak and teach, but I'm not sure what, where, or how. Money is becoming an increasing concern. I keep falling back on remembering the universe is abundant and will bring me what I need.

I'm blessed with several friends who come to the island over the spring, which allows me to relax the reigns of being in constant creativity, thinking, planning and wondering mode. I take stock of my contracted interior and hope the summer comes with more expansive answers.

I still have so many questions: I've slowly assembled a lot of puzzle pieces about why I've been called to this island, but I'm still searching for my bigger picture.

I spend a lot of time reflecting on the fact that creating a heart-based, spirit-inspired business from scratch is no joke. I underestimated the amount of work, perseverance, determination and grit it would take. Or the amount of time it would take to become known. I feel lost in the shuffle of all the other voices and offerings out there, and I feel irrelevant.

It's hard on my identity and sense of purpose.

The guava berries ripen, summer florals bloom, the heat is on, and I wonder, and I wander, considering how sometimes a vision can feel so clear, while other times the path feels obfuscated and we can't see through our mists.

I sometimes feel like the story of Noah and his arc. I think about how he must have felt constructing a giant boat when there was nary a drop of water to be seen. Did he struggle with faith? Was he aware he looked crazy to other people who didn't understand what spirit had told his heart? Did he ever wonder if he was crazy himself?

Sometimes I feel a little crazy. I know, to some, it may sound a little crazy to say I was told by spirit to move to an island and wait for what would show up there. Then I was given a bigger vision — my version of an ark — so I began to build it. So far, it's just sitting there unused, and I struggle to reconcile the truth of my inner world with the reality of my outer world.

Have I missed the metaphorical boat?

I struggle with feeling resentful at the universe. Part of me feels like a demanding child throwing a temper tantrum, "I did the big scary thing! I gave up my old life to come here! Why is it so hard? Why aren't you making it easier? Tell me my next step! I know you're capable of visions, magic and miracles, so where the hell is mine?"

I decide to keep going back to the basics whenever I get in these tricky feeling states: Nature. Grounding. Small steps. Sticking with myself. Tea and tarot. Deep breaths. Embracing uncertainty. Allowing my expectations and egoic mind to break against life's shores and be in a naked space of not knowing and vulnerability.

I try and remember I've always had clarity for my journey when the time is right, so if the clarity isn't there then the time is not right. I'm ready to gallop, but it's not time to be let out of the gate yet. I don't know why the delay, but I do know if it's not happening then it's not meant to... whatever 'it' is.

How strange to walk around searching for a missing piece that nobody else knows is missing but you, which means you are the only one who can find it and know if it fits.

Mostly I try and ground back into the island. Do the whole *be here now* thing. Practice the things I write about. Trust. Yield. Surrender. Receive. Ask for divine guidance. Pay attention to what shows up. Get out of my head and into my soul. Allow myself to be supported by the earth and rest my weary, battered heart.

66

Taurus Season

Invites us
to fall in love
with the earth,
be a creature
of naked belonging
and sweet vulnerability —

Who rests in
the truth of the
trees and the
wisdom
of the seas
and sun's daffodil
joy-filled jubilee.

Inviting us
to be,
receive,
dream,
believe —

In the goodness
of earth's grace,
under faith of
new moon's face;
be in soulful union
with the beauty
of this space.

67

SURRENDER, THEN SURRENDER AGAIN

*T*hese things I learned this last season.

I keep thinking everything is going to happen faster than it's really happening, and I'm beginning to realize this is an endurance race. Not a sprint.

Every time I think something is going to happen and explode me into a bigger version of self, it doesn't. Then I end up disappointed, and disappointment leads to disillusion, disillusion leads to self-doubt, and self-doubt leads to tripping and falling out of my flow.

When life threatens to pull you under and you are swimming in the sea, feeling stress pull at your ankles and weigh you down: *You must learn how to become the ocean.*

Not only do we choose our perspective, but we choose our paradigm — the onus of shift is entirely upon us and within our ability to create.

The universe isn't happening to us, it's creating with us, which is why it's extremely important not to let somebody else's relationship with the universe become your own.

If I'm not creating from a heart-space of joy, then I've lost my way and need to bring myself back to the core of who, what, and why I'm about in this world, without worrying about the how.

Trust is a quantum relationship extending horizontally, vertically, and all around. You can't trust in one area and doubt in another — it's interconnected. You either trust the universe will support you or you don't.

Let go of the plan. Let go of the how. Let go of the when. Surrender. Then Surrender Again.

Fire Within Me

To be a bright
light
and hold space
for the light,
and in so doing —
awaken
the light
in others.

68

LION HEART

My dear lion heart,
don't you know —
it all unfolds
according to the
patterns of your soul.

In polka-dot waves
and plaid idiosyncrasies;
through signs and shades
and cosmic synchronicities;
your tesselate tapestry
weaving the way
to the intricate path
of your soul's galaxy.

My dear lion heart,
I know you think
you still have a
way to go:

But stop and find ease
for how far you've stepped,
and know your journey
is already whole.

Your magnitude
of exactitude
will tell you
don't rest when
the currents mid-flow.

But I say *pause*
and watch the clouds
shift...
then drift
lift & sift

'long the current's
blue tow.

My dear lion heart,
you'll sow
then you'll grow
and in the end, all leads
back to your soul.

Whose rhythms
and rhymes
and triangle beats,
chime with the time
of your wandering feet
 — who walk in a line
of invisible belief —
following your shine
and letting heart lead.

So, don't be worried
that you'll miss the boat,
or lose your way,
or that life will withhold
the future dreams
you'll embody and own:

Because don't you know,
my dear girl, it all unfolds
according to the patterns
of your soul.

69

52 Weeks, Part II

*M*emorial Day Weekend 2019. It's a nostalgic weekend in the sense it harkens memories of BBQs, long weekends, camping, buying flowers for the garden, ice-cream cones, and all the best things that evoke anticipatory excitement for the summer season.

It's an auspicious weekend in the sense the Tuesday after Memorial Day 2016 was the day I drove to work, vowing to myself I would only spend 52 more weeks in Alaska. I fervently promised myself this time the following year I would have my practice closed and we would be moving to Kauai.

As it turns out, it took exactly 57 weeks from that day to manifest the move. However, the spirit of my intent stuck. I drove to my office the Tuesday after Memorial Day 2017 with a feeling of lightness that came from the knowledge — I did it. I stayed true to my vow to free myself. I only had four more weeks to work, then it was all about to change.

Change it did. Memorial Day 2018 was spent in Kauai at my parents. Our original upstairs neighbors were moving out that day, the new ones began moving in that same night, and we were three days away from finding out Sam had cancer. Life was a strange orbit of shifts and drifts, and we were trying to find firm footing while the satellites of our lives continued to transit.

Here it is one year later, and life is still rearranging and reforming. New pieces have come into the picture, we are further along than last year, and I feel like I am finally just starting to sink into what this move to Kauai is all about.

When I first arrived, I knew I was called to a deeper purpose of soul. I had followed my calling to the island and expected things would begin to manifest, which helped me make sense of that deeper purpose. I'd stumble onto new intuitive clients and start getting booked with readings. Maybe I'd intersect with a local shop owner who wanted to collaborate, and I'd slowly develop a reputation as a healer and guide.

Or perhaps one of my books would hit. Or one of my courses would take off. Or somebody would hear me speak and offer greater opportunity.

None of those things happened, and I've now realized that I was thinking about it all backward. I expected my work to shape and define me and help create the next step I was meant to take. I thought somehow what I was *doing* would inform my *being*, and the path would flow from there.

What I have learned since is: *I wasn't called here to do something first. I was called here to first learn bigger and deeper ways to be.*

Be in relationship with myself.

Be in relationship with the island.

Be in relationship with the universe.

Trust. Surrender. Release the plan. Release the how and the what.

Focus on the why: *To be a bright light and hold space for the light and in so doing awaken the light in others.*

I know my why. I wrote the above words a couple of weeks back, as I went into a deep space of regrouping and recalibration. May was a month of learning to come back home to myself and face the fact: how I thought things were going to look is not how things have been.

It was a month of learning my soul purpose isn't something I am going to do; it is who I am called to BE. When I bring myself back to my heart and let whatever I create flow from my center — when I focus on my light — I'm golden.

It brings new meaning to living my life from the inside out. I'm realizing in more profound ways my work has to come from my heart. That's where my true fire lays, and if I don't keep it carefully tended, stoked, and burning with the pure flames of light and love — then, anything else I try to launch into the world is going to burn up.

I realize this is what it means to be refined by the fire: *to keep alchemizing all of my experiences into wisdom, light and love, so I stay in deepest alignment with my heart path and truth.* After all, wisdom and enlightenment mean nothing if we can't learn to integrate and embody them into our being, so those lessons become a natural extension of who we are.

This is where I find myself this Memorial Day weekend. Far away from that girl who fervently uttered *52 weeks!* in 2016. Far away from the girl in 2017 who was tiredly, but triumphantly five weeks away from moving to Kauai and pulling off the biggest change of my life.

Far away from the girl of a year ago, who was still churning with questions over who she was and what she is called to Kauai to do. The girl who was about to have her heart broken upon the rock of Sam's loss, travel through another grief journey and come out the other side on new shore.

Those experiences may feel far away, yet all of those versions of self, needed to be seen and understood to bring them deeper inside and integrate them into my being, so I could keep moving forward.

I see myself spiraling with the universe somedays. Wrapping farther into myself. Circles, waves and spiers of truth, which dive me deeper into the universe within, as I expand in accord into the universe without. My energy becomes a force extending through me, around me, outside of me. Multidimensional in nature.

During those times of greater awareness, I know I don't need to worry about any of my questions of self. I just have to say *yes* to life's invitation back in 2016 to take this leap of faith and dive in. And I did, I did say *yes*. Every time I've come to a Y in the road, I find a way to say *yes*, to stay the course, to trust in what I cannot see — and there's no more reassurance I require than that to know:

It will all unfold as it was always meant, and I will have every-thing I truly need for my soul.

70

OBI-WAN AND THE ANCESTORS

I 'm proud of you Little Sister. The work you're doing is valuable and worthwhile, keep doing it.

You have a lot of growth ahead of you. Trust that you're perfectly supported in this growth. Listen to your own advice on intuition so you don't get in the way of your own growth.

Be joyful. You're on the right track with doing what brings you pleasure. Don't worry about money — it will keep showing up in your life and taking care of itself.

Remember, I'm like Obi-Wan now: *Luke, I am with you always. The force is strong in you.*

That was a joke Little Sister. Laugh. Smile. Be lightened. Call on the energy of the ancestors when you need support, they are here to help you too.

I know your heart is heavy, but if you could see what I see you would know all will be well. Try and override your head with your heart, and you'll know this to be true too.

71

GRIT & GLITTER

*W*hen life doesn't go your way, it doesn't mean you've got it wrong. It just means it's time for creative adaptation and soul transformation.

When the world is spinning and you're standing still, or you're spinning while life seems on pause; know life moves counter-clockwise at times and is still gently moving you towards exactly where you need to be. We live in a place of quantum possibilities, so let yourself be quantum.

When your season of grief has gone beyond what seems bearable, know you are seen and held by powers unseen. Your heartaches and life-breaks are being poured into by love's strange mysteries. Turn your teary eyes and hopeful palms to the sky and receive the light of grace and ease.

When you feel misunderstood, undone and undid, do know, dear soul, those spaces of being missed are the grist, in the sand, which seed and pearl our heart's growth.

The vulnerability of human is where we find our real; the grit and glitter of our ups and downs is how we follow the truth in our feels.

So, let angel songs grace all that seems wrong, and be at peace in the throng of life's upside-down songs. Still your heart and listen: *This is the space you will always belong; all you need do is go within to be in the truth of love's strong.*

72

I Carry Us Inside of Me

Sooner or later each of us has to realize that we live on a planet of transience, so we can't take it with us.

But what we can do is pour what we've loved best into our heart, so it becomes a part of our essence, becomes a part of our soul.

And we'll take that love wherever we go: *from here to the other side and back again, because the love in our soul holds the truth of our home.*

73

LOVING OURSELVES WHOLE AFTER LOSS

*M*y brother would have been 43 this week. His birthdays are a strange event for me. Every year that another one passes; I move further along a timeline without his physical presence and wonder who he would have been if he'd lived to see that age.

We lost Brent at 39. I was 38 at the time. My life was well-formed. Now I'm 41, soon to be 42. Still reforming life after grief's deconstruction dissolved the old version of myself.

Grief will do that to you. Dissolve who you once were, challenging you to become somebody new.

Losing Brent irreversibly changed me, and I'm still learning the nature of my own change. I remember walking around like half my lungs were ripped away for a long time, feeling broken inside, wondering if I'd ever feel whole again.

I don't know quite when it happened. Somewhere over the last 3 ½ years, new cells and tissue formed themselves around those rips and twined their essence through the blank spaces inside of me. This process formed bigger ways of breathing, which wouldn't have been possible if not for the empty space caused by loss.

Brent has become a part of my blood and limbs in ways that exceed my ability to put to words. The essence of who he's become to me is wordless. It can only be felt through heart's resonance and experience. I have a profound awareness that as my life force reaches and grows taller, like a giant Tree of Life, the transformative energy which came from losing Brent is woven throughout my bark and branches.

Magnificent scarlet blooms have opened, watered by an ongoing sense of his presence and the unconditional joy and immense love he now brings to our relationship.

Loving yourself whole after loss doesn't look the way you think it would.

We never go back to the shape we were or pick up the threads of the life we were living. There's too many broken strands, new colors, and interruptions in the pattern to reweave it as it was before. We can try to pick up where life left off, but grief has a rather pressing presence, which tends to require our attention sooner or later.

I gave it my full attention when it arrived in my life. My grief was so pressing I didn't see any other choice than to yield to the sorrowful, unexpected direction life had taken and lean into my heartbreak. It was an overwhelming break with many disorganized pieces.

Some of those pieces were permanently scattered by the wreckage of 2016. Some of those pieces became the catalyst for fierce self-examination, inviting me to retrieve and transmute my shards, under the light of grief's strange alchemy, in such a way that permanently changed my shape.

I became bigger. Braver. More grace filled. More perspective laden: I was a 38-year-old psychologist grappling with the grittiest bits of loss, while simultaneously having transcendent experiences with my brother in the afterlife.

How could this not reshape my perspective and help me see the world through a new lens of sincerity and love?

I became stronger. Deeper. More authentic. Hungrier for my life: I began to see the only thing standing in my way and holding me back from actualizing my dreams was myself.

I became aware. Achingly, keenly aware of the brush of trees on my face. The beat of earth beneath my feet. The breath of the sky and the massive amount of sentience radiating through life's veins. It felt like a love letter from the universe, and Brent was there in each page.

When I stripped it all down and distilled our relationship to what was most important at the core: the only essence that mattered was love.

I wish I could better describe what I mean by love.

Describe how love acted as the gateway that still connected me to Brent on the other side, simultaneously washing over, forgiving, and dissolving any bumps, edges, and ridges in our relationship as siblings in this life.

I wish I could describe what it was like the first time I felt his spirit. Or how it is now when I'm thinking about him and a presence will come close to me so strongly that I know he's right by. Or what it's like to feel him at family gatherings:

Set a place for me at the party Little Sister, and I will be there.

I wish I could describe the bittersweet light of what it's like to hold grief in one hand, the aching loss of what will never be, even as I hold hope and beauty in the other. I move forward knowing my life doesn't look the way I thought it would. Yet it's also turned into an authentic, creative expression of my being, which keeps evolving in ways more beautiful than I could have possibly imagined prior to 2016.

I wish I could describe these things, but I've learned the past few years these kinds of matters are best experienced and understood with the heart. The heart speaks a language beyond words and invites us to a vast space of healing and mending when we listen and heed its wisdom.

Loving myself whole after loss is a different process than I thought it would be. I'm a different shape than I ever would have expected. Yet my shape only exists, because of how Brent's love changed and rearranged me, and because I kept my heart open and gave myself over to the arrangement.

The writer in me wants to end this with some deep new wisdom, but I believe I've already said what I need to say most. So, I'm going to defer to the words of my 2016 self, who somehow found a way to navigate the grief journey with integrity, vulnerability, and transparency — and emerge on the other side whole.

2016-year-old me knows so much about the power of love, and I will spend the rest of my life honoring her wisdom.

Nobody's grief passage will ever look the same, but for me, after the jagged mountains, the desolate wasteland, the relentless desert, that deep long ocean of sadness, I washed up onto new shore.

Gradually got my feet underneath me and remembered I knew how to walk. Stepped out onto a landscape of gentle, shimmering pink where billions upon billions of stars light the way in the night, and the sun brings warmth and renewal each day. And I could see the invisible, gossamer strands of love running through it all. Wrapping everything together, connecting us in our shared humanity, holding us in place in the grace of this space.

Love has no walls here.

The possibilities are infinite.

74

About Brent

*I*f you want to know who Brent was and is to me, then just look at me. You will see him when you see me, because he has become such a deep part of my being that I live out the truth of his loss and his spirit in everything I do.

He taught me about the brevity of life. I can't think of any other catalyst which would have stopped me dead in my tracks, ignite me to quit my day job, move to a tiny island in the middle of the South Pacific, and follow a deeper path of heart, soul and truth.

He taught me about release and regeneration. I felt huge pieces of me missing after his loss, but the gift of going through that kind of a breaking is the ability to let go of all the stuff that doesn't matter and hang onto and grow the stuff that does.

He taught me to shine so much bigger than my fears. Yes, at times, it has been difficult, challenging and scary to start over at mid-life and allow myself space to go through this process of reinvention and transformation.

But you know what was more challenging. *Walking up to the podium to give his eulogy. Those initial 6 months after the loss where I couldn't feel the sun shining. Turning around and writing a book about it and staying open and vulnerable to elucidating that emotional territory.*

Whenever I feel fear, uncertainty and doubt over my path I think of that brave girl of 2016, and this voice speaks up in my head: 'C'mon little sister this is your life. LIVE it. Go BIG. Grab onto it with both hands and bring in all the love you can.'

That's what I've done. Every time I've had the chance to step out of the water back onto the certitude of shore, I've dived in deeper instead.

So, if you want to know who Brent is to me. Then just look at me. Because I now carry the best parts of who he was and who he's become inside of me. All the best parts are love by the way. They always were and forever will be.

For that, I am immensely grateful.

75

DREAM-SEEDS

I was walking on the Kapaa bike path earlier today, and this gorgeous hibiscus kept waving at me, trying to get my attention. So, I stopped for a minute to say hello and listen.

'Protect the seeds of your dreams,' she said.

Which deeply resonated with me, since I was deep in contemplation over how life has changed since we came to the island almost two years ago.

Two years ago, I had brand new seeds and baby dreams, and I quickly learned that just like a newborn, *our dreams are not for everyone's touch and eyes.*

They are for our own beings to nourish and nurture and bring to fruition. We get to share the fruit as we choose, but the origins of growth are vulnerable. Careless words, negative energy, and energetic zings damage and drain.

Something I've learned over the last couple of years is not to let somebody else's relationship with universe/higher power/energy/spirit become yours.

Don't take on their lack of belief.

Or fear of failure.

Or what ifs.

Or clouded vision.

Especially don't expect them to see your authentic heart if they are not invested in seeing their own authentic heart.

We have to take our heart-visions and soul-speak seriously enough to guard them with sacred care and only allow in what nourishes their flourish.

Protect the seeds of your dreams. Water them with clear intent and purpose. Root out weeds often. Feed them with joy.

Know that nobody else can nurture them but you, so don't expect them to. Though do know that the right people will come along and smile sunshine on you and be supportive of your soul truth.

Remember, if you've got a dream, it's because it's been given to you to create and crystallize. It wouldn't be in your heart to hope, yearn, and grow if it wasn't yours to actualize.

76

Deep Sea Diving

*I*f you are waiting for somebody to come along and give you permission: Here it is. Do it. Whatever that means for you. It's time.

If you are waiting for somebody to tell you it's okay to be brighter: Here it is. The world is calling for your supernova. Shine, diamond, shine.

If you are waiting for somebody to tell you it's all going to be okay: Here it is. It will. You have to trust. That's hard, I know. But it's the only way to soul-align and that is what it means to be in relationship with the divine.

Know it's going to be imperfect. Know you may not feel ready. Know it might not go as planned. Know that's totally okay. If we're sitting around waiting for perfect and ready, we will never move from where we're seated.

Don't wait for somebody else to do it for you. Step into it instead. Give yourself permission to become more, to claim your space, to speak your truth, to use your voice, to flex your limbs and take up the space you've been given.

Be your permission-giver and light-bringer and change-maker and things-shaker. Allow it to unfold in its messy, elegant splendor, embrace the call within —

And dive in.

77

END OF JUNE BLUES

*T*oday was a rough one. Parts of it were a struggle, a struggle I'm resisting, because I want so badly for life to feel good again after all the ongoing ups and downs.

This week is strange to begin. Convergence seems to happen at the end of June for me where one cycle ends, and another begins. I don't know if this is wrapped into the illuminating power summer solstice brings. If it's because June marks the halfway point of the year and my birthday follows in July, so old energies begin to burn up to usher in the new. If it's some other moon cycle or planetary cycle, or if the timing is coincidence.

What I do know is the end of June usually brings tower energy into my life, which shakes up and shakes out my bedrock.

Nine years ago, my divorce was finalized at the end of June. I remember not knowing how to feel, so I carried balloons up a mountain and symbolically released them as I vowed to live well, free, and seize the opportunity to deeply know and love myself. I woke up the next day feeling like I was free-falling through air, blank and scared with the realization I no longer had a safety net and had just ventured into unknown terrain.

The next few summers had their own kinds of convergence happening at the end of June. I was learning a lot about growing up, relationships, and what it really meant to live life from the heart and choose love. Love-break and heart-hurt happened twice at the end of June for me, and I was forced to grow beyond a more naive version of self and see the world through the wise eyes of a woman who learned not to outsource her power and strength to others.

Summer of 2017, I closed my private practice. Today marks two years from that day. Last summer, sweet Sam was declining rapidly and only had a few days left with us.

This year? Nothing as tragic, dramatic or life-altering occurred, but I sent the rent check in, and though things have been tight since we've been on the island, this is the first-time paying rent almost drained the bank account. There is nothing left: no hidden savings or fallback.

One of my biggest fears since we moved has been this day. I've always prayed and said, "I don't think I can handle the stress of not always having at least one month's rent in the bank. Please provide enough for us to have that." For a while, it worked. But not this month.

It's a precarious space to be. One I haven't been in for years. My identity as a professional woman is taking a beating, and I don't understand why the monetary streams which were keeping things afloat seem to have dried up. Hardest is struggling with knowing I put myself in this position by daring to follow my heart out of private practice and into my dreams of spiritual and creative entrepreneurship.

I've teetered back and forth between "just keep trusting" and fear throughout the day. My fear is bigger than just the fear of not having enough. It is the fear of being a personal and professional failure. It is the fear I should have accomplished whatever it is I came here to accomplish sooner. It is the fear I got it wrong, or I'm doing something wrong and not in "alignment," or else I would be manifesting more work.

The emotions are sticky and real today. It's Cancer Season, and I feel like a crab, hiding out in my shell, not quite sure which way to go, nor what to feel.

I find myself walking Frodo on the Kapaa bike path in the afternoon. Slightly drizzly and misty, it's uncharacteristically gray, which matches my mood just fine. When the rain comes, I take off my special Sam locket, so it won't get wet, and it ends up falling on the ground and breaking open. His picture and hair tuft spill out and I scramble to retrieve them while crying and wondering why everything feels like it's falling apart.

I feel so exposed with nothing to hide behind; my old identity is being stripped in a way I didn't anticipate. I didn't expect things to get this bare and thin. Old fears are being triggered, even though I've spent the last year trying to build a new way. It's a true test of spiritual beliefs about the words I've written numerous times: *we have a choice about the paradigm with which we view life.*

I feel like I'm doing battle in my mind between the old and the new.

The old paradigm says I should be scrambling and figuring out how to pull in new work straight away. Reevaluate my plans (because they're clearly not working as evidenced by my bank statement). The old paradigm wants me to give into anxiety and try super hard to make things happen to assuage myself and reassure myself I'm still on the right path, still the master and commander of my life.

The new paradigm says be still. Trust. All is not as it seems. You never were truly in control. This is here to teach you that, so don't make things mean something they don't mean. Don't forget you placed your trust in the hands of the universe — and now you want to grab it back into your own hands? *Whose hands do you think are bigger and more capable?*

It's a difficult space to be. There is a tension between the old way: taking charge of my life. Compared to the new way: charging my life to the power of LIFE, while still maintaining a presence as a co-creator and co-participant.

For today, I suppose co-creation means learning to be in the discomfort. I have no immediate fixes, solutions, or ability to make things happen faster than they are. Instead, I am left with awareness, dissolution, and asking that my needs be met in this tender-vulnerable space.

I am tender-vulnerable. I feel naked before Life in this moment, dependent upon divine guidance, direction and protection. It's an extremely uncomfortable feeling.

I wonder who I'll become in my need?

78

ANGEL TALK

*I*t is in this space of darkest feels, where my heart is cracked against stress's heel. I rage and I weep while my confidence shrinks and peels.

Somewhere in this broken place, a light breaks through with celestial grace, my heart undone, my soul unlaced, and the angels start to sing. *I hear them, not just feel them, with crystalline clarity for the messages they bring.*

Ariel, Jophiel, and Gabriel surround me. Michael stands watch and Uriel helps transform me. Raphael heals with skills and feels. Haniel says I must learn to trust the deep mysteries and know the moon's wise tools.

It is precious, this gift, and I let myself drift. Broken in being. Spirit rich. I'm not alone while my troubles twist, spin, and sift. I lean in and let the angels carry, speak, and lift.

They tell me to trust and return to the light within; there is where my answers exist.

79

JOPHIEL'S JUBILATION

*L*ook for the light in all things. It may not always be easy to find, but you have to realize you are the diamond, you are the pearl, you are the light.

You are the light in all things.

You are the common denominator.

You are the light that shines bright.

Can you see how beautiful you are, dear star?

You are so loved.

80

RETROGRADE

*I*f June was for the blues, then July sinks midnight deep.
It's eclipse season, and I feel eclipsed by stress, sorrow and confusion, as I wonder why things have become so hard.

My current circumstances have forced an unanticipated spiritual and identity crisis. My finances are terrifying, no new work is showing up, and I feel like a professional and personal flop. I thought I came to Kauai to fulfill my path of soul, and I'm so confused as to why everything is devolving.

Intuitively, I feel like I'm being blocked by something I can't see, like this is happening for a reason, but I can't understand why or how this will serve my highest good.

I truly thought my path would be clear by now and opportunity would present itself to find the growth I seek. I don't know if I've missed the path, or lost my way, or if I can actually trust my intuition that everything actually is unfolding according to my soul's path, and even these harsh circumstances have a purpose for the great whole.

I want to believe that. At times it feels impossible with zero evidence of success and a thin thread of hope. I feel like I'm going backwards in my life and failing to self-sustain as an adult.

Astrologically, it's not just eclipse season, but retrograde season as well. Mercury, Saturn, Jupiter, Neptune, and Pluto are all in retrograde right now. Retrograde means the movement of the planet slows on the ellipses, giving the illusion it's moving backwards. It is not in fact moving backwards, it's just that while it's slowing, everything else continues at its usual pace, creating a backwards illusion.

Retrogrades offer opportunity for recalibration and realignment. On the surface, it might look like things are malfunctioning, breaking down, and going wrong. Yet underneath the surface, tectonics are often moving that align us in deeper ways. Often when planets leave retrograde, we will suddenly have a fresh insight or burst of clarity about our lives and our journeys, and we will feel inspired, renewed and empowered to move forward with greater purpose.

It occurs to me that maybe I'm in retrograde right now as well.

Maybe my external circumstances are creating an illusion of stagnation, while I watch others around me excel, expand, and move forward in their lives.

Maybe I'm tied up so I can realign. Maybe everything happening on the surface gives the illusion I've gone backwards in my life. Quit my job, lost my income, lost my old identity… but when the time is right, I will surge forth with a giant burst of aligned movement.

Maybe the only way to accomplish my dreams is to take the hit I'm going through right now. The hit to my pride, my finances, and my sense of identity. Perhaps on a soul level, I've always known this time is coming, and my soul said to my heart: "This is going to hurt a little, but I promise it's going to be okay. It is all happening exactly as it needs, and you are going to agree whatever is waiting on the other side is well worth it.'

I don't know what else to do, so I pray, I show up as I can, and I hope.

I return to my intuitive tools daily, sometimes multiple times a day, and use that space as a way to listen to my soul and re-center myself.

I begin teaching Intuitive Writing Workshops at a local shop and, though just a handful of women show, it feels like a friendly step of expansion in a difficult time; it's a ray of light.

I listen to the angels and straddle two worlds. The things I'm told in the etheric lift me up and lighten me, but the heaviness of my circumstances still weighs on my heart no matter how many times I'm told to trust.

I have a sense of unspooling; something inside of me is once again being undone. My emotions feel messy and disorganized. I don't feel like myself. I feel lost a lot and punctuate that with trying to do what I can to show up for my creative work.

Mostly I still feel like I'm searching for something. I don't know what it is, but I feel myself looking for my missing puzzle pieces each day, trying to understand the bigger picture of my calling.

My heart feels flattened. I'm struggling to find joy, but I try.

I try and hang onto hope. I'm being fully stripped of my old identity. I can no longer use the past to inform my sense of who I am now, and my old devices for having a sense of control, agency, provision, and power have been shattered.

Maybe that's exactly how my soul wants it.

I don't know what else to do except to surrender to life's tide and see where it carries me. I realize I'm sitting squarely in the palm of the universe with no choice except to trust my being and becoming to the divine and stay open to whatever is trying to unfold in my soul in these challenging times.

81

YOUR HEART IS MAGIC

I like to think of each of us as Cosmic Investigators. Soul Explorers. Heart Adventurers. Who get to play Scooby-Doo with the cosmos, as we search for the clues that resonate in our heart and piece together our bigger picture of soul.

Our life then becomes a patchwork of silk scraps, love notes, and starry truths, which help us make sense of who we are and what our purpose is in this lifetime.

One thing I've learned is purpose is multilingual and open to many interpretations. It's not about one set path, it's about who we are, the choices we make on a daily basis, and how we choose to direct our energies.

After all, there are many ways to be a light. Or to be a motivator for peace. Or to be an unruly heart, who does things backward and out of the book, yet still states an elegant case for the cause of love.

Purposes are like the stars. There are billions of them, which means there are billions of ways to shine bright and light up the night.

Don't stop listening to the feelings whispering and calling to you. Follow them. Put on your spyglass and take a closer look at the things that make your heart sing. Collect those experiences and tapestry them together into the bigger picture of you, even if they don't make sense.

They don't need to make sense to your mind, they already make sense to your heart.

Allow yourself the grace to be a Topographer of the Universe. Take notes on the pages of your heart of everything you find and see. You're not foolish for seeking more: you are big, bold, beautiful, intuitive *and your heart is magic.* Hang onto that and let that knowledge be your boon travel companion.

Trust yourself. Trust your heart. And you can always trust your magic.

82

ROSE IN WINTER

*D*on't worry little sister. Everything will happen in its own time.

Usually, the rose blooms in summer, yet sometimes the rare rose blooms in winter when hope is needed most.

You must learn to be like the wintertime rose Little Sister. You'll bloom when this world needs it most.

83

UNPETALING

My dear one,
I know the struggle is real,
sometimes there's
a divide between
the mind and the heart,
which tells you to believe
the fear over the love.

It is a strange thing
this life: we move through
it in accordance to what
we're first taught,
then growing up allows
us to become more true.

We learn to open in the
process, unpetaling
like a rose as our heart
seeks to bloom.

I cannot take the struggle away,
and my dear one, I know
you're ready to release the pain,
but this I can gift to you
to help ease the way —

Your heart is a storyteller
of words untold.
words which speak love
in drenched fistfuls
and silken breath.

The pain you feel is
the wound and the balm;
your soul is a wild
creature who feels
to your bones.

Fleets of angels call you their own.
Find the love, and you'll find your way home.

84

NEW BREEZE

*T*he sun is peeking through the dappled jungle green, the family is still sleeping tucked into a cozy bundle of human and fur, and I've been quietly sipping coffee and contemplating turning 42 today.

It wasn't that long ago I was contemplating turning 40.

We'd just arrived on the island, and it felt like a nice solid number to build a new foundation on. I remember sitting by the ocean, down in Kapaa, the evening before July 27, 2017, thinking about how remarkable it was that I had actualized my dream of coming to this island.

Since we just passed our 2-year island anniversary, I've also been thinking a great deal about all that's transpired these past 48 months: How I thought things would be over here and how they actually are. Who I was then and who I am now. How I've changed, stretched and grown. The unexpected struggles and hardships that have occurred, and the beautiful and magical things that have occurred as well.

Earlier this week I wrote a piece where I likened Kauai to the Mr. Miyagi of islands.

You come to her eager to learn, thinking you're ready for the next step. Then she puts you to work making you learn how to wax on and wax off for such a long time, you begin to wonder exactly what you're doing here, if you've made a mistake coming, and where she's leading you.

But something else I have learned on this island is that the soul of Mother Kauai is the soul of a Master Healer, Teacher and Empath.

Like any good Yoda-Master-Teacher, she only gives you what you need to know in that particular moment. She knows greater wisdom comes with patience, skill, time, and learning to turn inwards. *She will reflect back to you what is brightest in you, what is darkest in you, and offer you the opportunity for deeper integration, self-exploration, and self-awareness.*

The past couple of years have felt like I signed up for another tour of duty with the heart of the universe. I feel naive as I write these words, but I thought the true test of faith was saying goodbye to my long-term life in Alaska and moving to the island.

I didn't think things would go perfectly when I arrived, but I did expect life to settle down and coalesce after the first 3–6 months. Instead, it's been a material and spiritual roller coaster of ups, and downs, and surprising corkscrews.

The other day I was having breakfast with my Dad, and I joked to him that these past two years made me feel like an ancient character in a Dickens novel. "It was the best of times, it was the worst of times," I said to him. Dad laughed, then said with a note of gravity, "You gave up everything to be over here BethAnne. Not many people would do that."

The sun is now muggy and full. My earlier reverie broken when the household woke up, and I took Frodo out for his morning walk along the winding country roads of our neighborhood.

It feels extra hot and sticky out, still and paused, with whispers of gently swishing clouds that hint at a new breeze on the cusp of breaking through. Cooling things down and sweeping clean any leaves or debris that are ready to let go.

It's a poignant metaphor for the last two years.

I did give up everything to come to this island. Home, job, income, security. Old identity, familiar friendships, familiar patterns, familiar anything. We lost our beloved Samwise. Even my marriage has been shaken up, shook out, and ironed into a new shape and season.

All those happenings were pieces I wasn't expecting: an ongoing onslaught of change, which has been emotionally and psychologically overwhelming at times.

There's been a lot of soul searching and questioning of my heart path in these moments. A lot of moments of reckoning where I've come face to face with myself, always with the same question: "Well BethAnne, what do you really believe?" Because I've begun to see that is what it comes down to. Belief.

Either I believe I'm following my heart and the calling of my soul and spirit will support me on the deeper, invisible path of the self. Or I don't.

I keep returning to this same crossroads time and time again. It's my personal crossroads of faith, which challenges me to take my faith and trust to a deeper level every time I stand at these roads and make a choice about which direction that I want to point my heart's compass.

I know if I choose to believe, then I can rest assured, trust, and know it's all leading me in the direction I want to go... even when it doesn't look like it. Such simple words to write, such hard words to live, but those moments of reckoning and wrestling with our truth are also where purification, consecration, and revelation happen.

What I see now — that I couldn't see two years ago (or even 6 months ago) — is: just because I deconstructed the physical structures of my old life to get to Kauai, doesn't mean the deconstruction process was over.

I moved the exterior elements of my old life, but I now know the universe had deeper plans for my interior: Old beliefs, old values, and old ways of being have all been slowly blown away. Replaced by something new and different.

More allowing, less forcing. More trusting, less having to know. More unfolding, less expectation. Angelic presence, spiritual growth, and a deepening of intuition. A few other things I can't quite put words to yet, because I'm still understanding them myself as I experience my own unfolding.

That's the thing about a new breeze — we won't know where it's blowing us until we arrive. Sometimes, though the answers may still feel far away, we are closer than we think. All it takes is one gust to travel us to our next step.

For today, my next step will be up the familiar red dirt trails of the Sleeping Giant, because despite the heat, we've decided to go hiking then go in search of the ocean and cupcakes. Other than that, I'm allowing the day to be whatever it will be having learned these last two years that I'm both the shaper and the shapee.

We lay our life's groundwork as best we can, then trust spirit's winds to meet us in there and help us understand and alchemize the composition of our own change.

166

85

Reseeding Our Soul

"All good things are wild and free."

It's true, I thought: Sometimes we must repattern, rewild, and reseed our soul. Learn to see disruptions as life's way of breaking us out of our daily stream of consciousness and giving us space to see things from a new lens, so we can be liberated from dead roots of self that no longer serve our highest growth.

We must return to the soil of self and beat with the wild of the earth, freeing ourselves from old paradigms, constraints and beliefs. Allowing ourselves to return to seed and dare to face the shock of new, so we can grow outrageous blooms.

"All good things are wild and free."

It's true, I thought: Nature. Love. Authenticity. Moonlight, Creativity, Imagination and Dreams. Wild and free and tinged with butterfly wings, and unicorn wisdom, and dragon tears, which create sacred pools where we can swim in between with the mysteries.

Nature returns, rewires, and rewilds: Need a friend, talk to a tree. Need a joy, talk to a flower. Need to ground, talk to the earth. Need to flow and let go, talk to the sea.

And if you need to release all that would weigh you down and shackle you to lesser things that don't reflect the divine truth of your soul?

Walk outside with bare soles. Or take a bath and let the water heal your soul. Let all be renewed and released as you remember in your heart the words of Thoreau:

"All good things are wild and free."

86

In the Palm

*M*aybe we're not supposed to know. As human as it is to yearn for certainty and the bigger picture.

Maybe the more daring, adventurous and engaged you are with the heart of the universe, the more engaged in mystery your life becomes. *As if the universe itself realizes you're not here to play it easy, you are here to play for keeps, because your heart refuses to leave this lifetime with any stone unturned.*

Perhaps that's what it truly means to be "in flow." To develop such a naked trust and vulnerability with the heart of this universe, that you release all structures that hold you in stasis and instead become free to live wildly. From one heartbeat to the next, trusting the path will unfold with every step of trust you take.

Living in the palm of the universe itself, being so tenderly cradled and gently led, you wonder how anybody could buy into the illusion of control, when it's so evident we are given help and support every step of the way.

There is deep abiding love in the palm. Guidance and reassurance. Magic and miracles, that you'd miss had you not stripped yourself to this deepest level of trust.

The palm is where you finally begin to realize that if "it" had come along and made everything "better" (by having things instantly make sense and snap into place), you would have continued to live a one-dimensional experience where X marks the spot and A + B always = C.

Yet that life is not for you, dear one. You were called to live quantum. To realize time is a circle and the universe manifests in cycles and waves.

This is the space where you can begin to learn that A + Z may very well open a hidden door, which takes you to a symphony of rainbow possibilities.

This is the space where you begin to accept a more fluid, shifting day-scape that changes often, arises unexpected feelings, and who's teaching you that the "It" (your bigger purpose) is finding the joy, magic, and hidden gems in the unfolding.

This is the space where you hold the energetic hand of God, and you say — *I'm sorry I ever doubted you were anything other than my friend.*

Angels will sing nearby. You'll surrender into a deeper level of trust than you could have ever imagined, as the universe brews its strange alchemy of divine timing and you believe in the face of uncertainty:

You will indeed become, who you've always felt called to be.

87

To See by Candlelight

I'm trying to learn what I can in this difficult season.

The other day, I was talking to a friend after our workout class. She is a kindred connection who sees life through a lens of hope, and we were having an honest conversation about how our summers were going. I shared the financial pressures and unexpected breakdown that has been occurring.

I don't remember how we arrived from Point A to Point B, which is usual for our conversations which can span great leaps in short bouts of time, but I do remember her saying (in regards, to my current circumstances):

"Well enjoy it! You'll never be in this space again, so you might as well see what gifts it brings you!"

Her words stick, and I realize, whether or not I want to be here, I'm back in a space of diving for the light. I need to go through my current depths to retrieve my pearls of wisdom and truth, so I can understand my life from a higher perspective.

It's Leo season, with fire being the element associated with Leo, and this feels an apt metaphor for life in this moment. Under summer's hot gaze I contemplate: what's burning away in my life right now? What is left as my old ideals, ideas, and self-image refine in the fire's flames?

What gifts of candlelight can I find to see me through this darkness of circumstance?

1. Life is glaringly present at the moment, which means I am glaringly present and achingly aware. It's a painful place to be; I can't escape myself, my emotions or my energy. Yet it is also a beautiful place to be, because my crystalline awareness is what is helping me to pick up on the subtle nuances and frequencies of energy, which help me sense spirit in clearer ways.

2. I don't like my mental chatter that says I'm failing and wasted my time, so I've been changing it by praying that none of my efforts or energies be wasted, but used to create unexpected side doors of possibility and opportunity that will be better than I imagined. After all, the universe isn't linear but multidimensional, which means the universe is creative enough to alchemize, upcycle, recycle, and constantly use our old ingredients to bring things into surprising form.

3. I realize I am doing what I set out to do on Kauai: *live a more intuitive, creative, spiritual life.* I have never been more in-sync with the cosmos than in this space of interdependency, receptivity, and need.

4. I have the gift of space and free time. My life has been decluttered of almost all my old work and obligations. I have the space to attend to myself and be present for myself in deeper ways, so I can better understand the nature of my soul and know myself in an abiding intimate way.

5. There are new seeds being planted within me, which I can feel taking root. I feel different internally, and I have an initial awareness something is shifting and replanting. I sense the first origins of steadfast self-respect and integrity, as I fully realize the scope of my choices and the extreme courage I've shown in following my heart and trusting life's process to this level.

At the time, these new seeds are only trickles of a dawning awareness. I do not know what they will grow into in the months to come, or how important they will become for my journey.

I do not know they are acorns who will become great oaks. I do not know many of my old roots are being severed, so these seeds have new room to take root. All I know at the time is a seedling perception of their origin and an intuitive sense something will eventually be birthed.

What are these seeds you might ask?

The beginning of truly understanding the depths of my heart's desire; old fears are being burned away which say I am not relevant, my work is not good enough, and I don't deserve to be fully seen.

The beginning of unleashing my authentic truth; old beliefs are being burned away, which keep me from speaking my full truth for fear of rejection, alienation, or judgment.

The beginning of unshakeable self-belief; old thoughts are being burned away, which keep me from fully embracing my new path and believing I have something of value to say.

The beginning of finally knowing unconditional trust; old stories are being burned away, which have kept me in an energetic holding pattern of constantly questioning if I can trust my process.

The beginning of a core affirmation of my unwavering commitment to the cause of love; my understanding of love is being transformed, refined, and purified — so I can be taken deeper into the heart of the cosmos, the heart of spirit, and the heart of my true self.

88

Gabriel's Incitation

*Y*ou must learn to see the beauty in yourself, so you can better see it in others.

Think how each star dazzles, yet also exists as part of a greater constellation. It's doesn't shine less bright because other stars exist. Instead, it shines all the brighter, happy to coexist and be in service to the whole.

Your light is your own to be freely given to others of your own accord. Go within to find it.

You are part of a great sea of light, both separate and whole. Use your light in service to the cause of love and you shall gain more light.

Remember the true light in your soul has never been and can never be dimmed. Allow yourself to shine from within.

89

PERMISSION TO SHINE

A voice floated in on a tangerine dream, confettied with flecks of white and gold: "It is safe to become and be seen as your highest expression of self."

Words of growth and change which say: *Trust is key when we are fully ready to commit to the sensitive knowing in our contrary hearts, who refuse to fit the boxes this world has carved out.* Trust can be hard; unpeeling fears like onions sheds our old skins and ignites us to live life from a deeply vulnerable space.

But this space is where your magic is found. This space is where your heart cries and soul sighs, sigh the loudest and can tip your life upside down in dazzling spirals of adventure and grace. *Should you have the courage to follow.*

Doubts are human and valid. Reluctance understandable in the face of brave change. Take all the time you need dear one, to go within and let the amber flames of your life force refine such things.

But please don't let yourself be steeped, stopped, or stepped by other's careless words and blind opinions, who judge what they do not see or know. Because they smothered their heart cries and souls sighs long ago.

You were meant to experience the world in celestial technicolor and symphonic symphony, bright soul. So, let yourself grow.

Let yourself move with the trees and listen to the music of the elven beats. Let yourself see the sky pink and hear the world in dreams. Let yourself keep tunneling into your most authentic, exquisite, soulful being.

If anyone should look at you, askance, keep on with your dance and joyfully say:

"It is safe to become and be seen as my highest expression of self."

90

ENOUGH FOR ALL

You can pray unceasing
through the act of breath...
allowing your mind to remember

— answers to prayers are
as prolific as the trees
(abundance the resolution
to fear & lack's illusion) —

There's room enough for
all to win when the world
lays down in love.

91

August Blessing

Sometimes we have those weeks with a lot of twists and turns where words fall into the convoluted cracks and our small spaces of still-pause-silence become extremely golden.

That's life sometimes, isn't it? Twisted and turned with cracks in-between, and we learn to anchor ourselves in the pauses. Cradle our moments of solitude, raindrops and grounding into whatever feels and heals our hearts as home.

We find ourselves again in those spaces. Tap into sacred laughter and gentler ways of being. Allow our ego-states to fall away, as we drop into deeper truths that bring us back to the light within and allow us to reconnect and rekindle.

If you've had one of those weeks, then I wish you ease.

If you're feeling fatigued, then I wish you rest.

If you're feeling grieved, then I wish your heart the comfort of 1,000 angel songs.

And if you're in need of joy, then I offer you this wisdom: *go find something that makes you laugh, because when we can find levity in the gravity all the heavens smile with us.*

Be good to you and cherish your soul. It holds the truth of who you are.

92

Red Thread

*R*ites of passage don't always look the way we think they will.
Often, the universe shapes the elements of our lives to create a rite of passage. We descend into our interior self, even as we live out our exterior steps, trying to make sense of the symbols, themes, and meaning going on.

It's as if the subconscious itself is made manifest, and instead of our inner world speaking in symbols whose language we see spelled out in the external world, the events of our external world become the symbols for understanding the language of our soul.

I wouldn't have chosen this particular rite of passage. It's made up of financial hardship, discouragement, and facing the reality that all the hard effort I've poured into trying to create a new business has yielded little tangible fruit.

I can't see the way through. Or how things will shift. Everything I've been taught about following our heart bliss and watching the universe respond with miracles, doesn't feel like it's held true... *yet*.

I cling to my '*yet*.' Cling to it like a small life raft in the middle of a storm. Cling to it like a cairn on a concealed path when I don't know which way to go.

I tuck my '*yet*' into my heart pocket and try and nourish it with seeds of hope and rivers of dreams, instead of despair. I'm over two years into my dream and I feel like I'm going backwards; the financial pressure is crushing and real, no matter how much I try and remind myself of life's abundance.

It is in this broken space that I become more in touch with my own brokenness.

It is in this broken space I'm forced to dig deeper. To dig, even beyond, the angel messages that comfort and surround. To dig deeper inside of me. Tunnel further into my heart cave.

I bring myself back to this space over and over, as if I'm lost in Minos's labyrinth and the red thread of Ariadne is how I'm keeping myself from feeling like I'll never find my way out.

The red thread is my heart, my cairn, my life raft and lifeline to love, my way through this dark rite of passage where I've now been asked to trust far beyond what I believed I was capable of trusting.

Trust is what my heart keeps telling me: *Trust just a little bit longer, a little bit deeper, a little bit wider. Don't give in to fear or desperation or thinking you've gone awry. Trust just trust. Do what you can as you wait, but trust.*

Somewhere in my red thread tangle of confusion, I feel a felt-sense rise up, like a word-dream, who speaks with a wisdom deep inside of me:

Your heart is becoming more alive and free.

93

CINNAMON DREAMS

September
falls different
in the tropics;
less sweaters
& pumpkin spice nice
more sweat &
hibiscus tea, iced.

Yet it's this time
of year,
that my heart
turns golden
thoughts
of cranberry sliced
with cinnamon dreams,
& symphonic geese
fly farewell
themes.

We learn
from the leaves
how to change
then release —
allowing old things
to fall free
to earth.

To seed, transform
& rebirth new love.

94

Harvest Moon

*I*t was a strange kind of summer. The kind that came with a few roller-coaster twists and turns, which felt like they went against the grain of what should have been easy, buttery days.

I'm coming to learn that's just life. Last summer we were grappling with losing Sam, this summer came with its own challenges. A lot of growth has happened within the pages of these two summers.

Now it's Fall. Well, it's Fall in my heart. We do live on an island, which means autumn is not the same for us as it is for most in the northern hemisphere — it's not usually until November that we begin to see temperature drops.

I can feel the crisp breeze in my interior anyway. As if some rugged, wild Alaskan part of me will always roam the cranberry tundra this time of the year. Peer down at ochre-fairy-tale-like mushrooms. Delight at the first gold touch of the leaves. *Even if those experiences only happen now in my spirit and mind.*

The trade winds are coming back to the island though. The guava berries are ripe and will begin to sprinkle the trails with crabapple red and banana yellow throughout September and October.

Football starts soon, and we'll be at my parents, wearing Pats gear, and using the game as a means to honor, remember and celebrate Brent's life.

The Harvest moon is coming soon, denoted by the full moon closest to autumn equinox. For anyone living in tune with nature's cycles, it's a natural time of the year to take stock and receive the bounty of the seeds you've been planting in life.

It's also time to think about the seeds you want to plant in the next cycle.

I'm still sifting through what that is for me, but I know I want those seeds to feel lighter, more gracious, and more appreciative.

I never expected to struggle so much on this island and to be stretched, challenged and grown so. Some of those challenges have robbed me of some of the lessons of my younger years, and I feel the call to return to my heart's roots and reclaim any territory I've ceded.

There was a time, somewhere back in 2012, that I think of as: *my post-divorce, single in my early 30's, finding myself again years.* In this season, I was reconstructing life and learning what it meant to fall in love with my life.

To be in a love relationship with life itself.

This was the time in my life where I learned the more you appreciate and value your life, the more your life will appreciate and value you.

My heart-center was wide open, and I suddenly felt connected to the world in a way I never had before. I was coming to a deeper understanding I was in a relationship with myself and the world around me. I'd often go to the park, sit on a bench with my loyal elder pup, Pepe, and talk to the sky in my heart.

Simple things made me happy. Books. Candles. Sandwiches. I begin to see myself as a creative being, who could bring a sense of artistry into my days by wearing playful clothing and developing an eye for finding beauty and extraordinary in the ordinary.

My feelings became gateways that led me to intuitive truths in myself. My art journal and blog became ways to process my experience of self, understand my own waters and flows, and tell my stories in a way that brought depth, color, resilience and truth to things, no matter the topic.

The moon taught me about phases, cycles, and how important it is to own our bright side and our dark side and see them as part of the whole. The mountains taught me about embracing the strength found in living wild, free and following my bellicose heart.

Mostly what I learned during this time was a deep sense of self-love. The importance of valuing my life, finding joy in the everyday and being a practitioner of appreciation and beauty. Hard things happened during this life season, but I'd poured so many truths of light into the soil of my soul I was able to navigate them and still maintain reverence for my life.

Here it is, 8 years later, and I feel called to take a few lessons from my younger self and bring back the wisdom I discovered in those years, so I can release and transform the bitterness, pain, and emotional suffering I've been feeling.

Allow myself to return to the basics of tending a happy heart and a happy life. Relax into an even deeper level of patience with whatever I'm creating in this phase of my life on Kauai. Redevelop a gaze of thoughtful joy and fairytale wonder.

Those are the seeds I want to plant this fall. I still have creative and prosperity goals, but I know those material things won't mean anything if the immaterial isn't anchored in grateful reverence.

Grateful reverence, like anything else, requires careful tending and energy lest it begins to wither and wilt. So, with that, I asked myself a question this morning:

What would happen BethAnne, if you made it your goal over the new few months to look for all the gratitude you can? What if you returned to the beauty way and found all the beautiful moments you could in each day? What if you made it a point to appreciate, even when things don't go as you thought?

Falling in love with your life is the only way to find peace in the change: this is when you're most connected to yourself. This is when you're most wise. This is how you return to the heart of where your true wealth resides.

95

ARIEL'S HEART CYCLES

I know your heart feels tired. Even lions go through winter seasons when they must conserve. All things move in cycles in accordance with the design of the Great Creative Being.

Don't fret child, whatever you feel you lost will also come back in new ways. In the meantime, *remember your true abundance comes from within.* Focus on my dominion to remember prosperity and wealth. Prosperity is nature's way, and you are part of the natural world.

Do not mistake this winter for the condition of your soul or your material existence. It's just a season that has its own gifts of stillness and slowing. Gather your harvest, see how much you've already planted. *Know it will grow in time in accordance with a higher map of soul.*

Do not be afraid. Look to me in lack, and I will help remind you how full your cup is. Call on me, Archangel Ariel, and I will help you return to the truth of your heart.

96

SOUL MUSINGS

*W*hat if all you did was ask the question, "Who would I become if I allowed myself to be my highest expression?"

Then you took a single first step, and in so doing, you ignited the dominos of your soul, who heard your words, knew your intent, then set into motion every single thing you'd need to be your highest self.

What if life isn't doing it to you. What if it's your soul. What if your soul, in its divine source intelligence, helped unfold all you need to self-actualize?

What if the chaos is really a storm come to cleanse, clear and reset all aspects of your being, so you can create a new channel of self?

What if it is all the doing of your soul? Not some outside force happening to you, but some inside force who is working with you. Who loves you infinitely and who heard your sincere commitment to become a fuller self, so they answered your commitment in the most unlikely way, bringing you the ingredients you would need to birth your dreams.

Maybe nothing is as it seems, and we must look beyond the illusion. Be like the moon who shines on all. See the truth waiting for us in the shadows. Realize the path to liberation can only be found through sieving away what no longer fits and allowing new skin to renew and redeem.

There is nothing more terrifyingly beautiful in this world than a soul living whole and free, and the only way to achieve that is for circumstances to unbind all bounds, so we become vulnerable and tender in our need.

Ready to release the old and rebirth ourselves free.

97

Trail of Becoming

"I was just thinking that of all the trails in this life there is one that matters most. It is the trail of a true human being. I think you are on this trail and it is good to see."
— *DANCES WITH WOLVES*

*T*he trade winds are blessedly back, blowing everything with them and some of the stagnancy and stuckness I've been feeling begins to shift.

I realize some things in those shifts:

My heart feels like it has been broken this last season in a new way. As if the compound effect of difficulties over the last couple of years caused a collapse, and I can feel the grief and pain that has dimmed me.

I am going through some deep spiritual process of change, which is taking longer than I expected, and the events in my life are being used by the universe to support me in divining my change.

Last, all of this is ushering me into a deeper space of self-love, self-acceptance, and knowing my heart in new ways.

The other night I was doing something I do best: tuck into bed, candle lit, incense burning, a stack of oracle cards and my journal.

Cards speak to me in a way I cherish. The images, the words, and the intuitive knowing that comes through when I work with them are treasured gems. They tell stories and act as doorways to the subconscious mind and deeper chambers of self.

If the universe speaks to us through patterns, numbers, symbols, signs and synchronicities, then cards can act as a vehicle to give us a direct line to communicating with the divine through tangible means.

"Help me understand my bigger picture and purpose," I said. *"Help me better see how this is all working together."*

I ask this question in multiple forms on a daily basis. Through breath and prayer and collecting the experience of the day, which jigsaws together another piece of my puzzle. I feel like I'm walking along my trail of truth with a lantern, seeking the path of knowledge, not quite certain what I'm looking for, not quite certain when I'll find it, nonetheless pressed upon to press on.

It's as if the bigger vision of the path has been obfuscated, and I wonder when I'll see a clearer fuller picture.

I know love has a lot to do with it. So does grief in its alchemical way. My relationship with the divine is wrapped around it all. My soul calling and career purpose and Kauai life are all so deeply intertwined, each one blends and bleeds into the other like an endless bed of red roses, which looks like one big rose if you were to travel up to the sky, sit on a cloud and observe the whole.

I talk to the angels all the time, and I feel their support and guidance. They cannot tell me the bigger mystery of myself, but they do give me pieces and perspective.

Gabriel encourages me to create with greater clarity by putting the intention in everything I do to awaken love in others.

Michael leaves me in tears with a new moon message that's so profound, I'm completely humbled at being the receiver of such words.

Chamuel says to think of him like a tether in the storm and to call on him when I feel untethered and need to have a sense of peace, comfort, and wellbeing.

The angels teach me we are never alone. Alone is the mistruth; surrounded and connected to love is the truth. I thought I already knew this truth, but something I'm learning about truth is you keep learning it in ways that burrow deeper into your being, unearthing layers of yourself who you are still learning.

Ariel tells me: *Truth frees in its entirety, because truth is alive in love. Truth evolves in love. Love always seeks to free itself to become a higher expression. So, keep freeing yourself from anything that is no longer your truth so you can become a higher expression in love.*

I contemplate the meaning of this and recognize this season of truth is taking me to the deepest places inside the roots of myself where my beliefs of trust, surrender, support and security exist.

I realize even though I thought I believed I was fully supported by Life; I had actually put a lot of conditions on that support:

I trust and believe I am fully supported by Life, *as long as* my bank account shows a certain amount.

I trust and believe I am fully supported by Life, *as long as* I feel successful in my career.

I trust and believe I am fully supported by Life, *as long as* I can see the path of how I'm going to get there.

I trust and believe I am fully supported by Life, *as long as* I have a firm sense of my identity and who I'm becoming.

I could fill a journal with the number of *as long as* that I've encountered and been challenged to surrender since I came to this island. I'm learning as I go that *as long as* creates a self-imposed limitation, and I am better served by releasing that phrase and replacing it with *and*.

I trust and believe I am fully supported by Life *and* I don't see the path.

I trust and believe I am fully supported by Life *and* I don't know how to move forward.

I trust and believe I am fully supported by Life *and* I don't know who I'm becoming.

It takes a lot of courage to face our and's.

I don't have it fully together these days. In fact, I think I've been a collection of broken pieces for a while. I've felt so messy, confused and lost, yet determined to keep showing up for myself while I vacillate with endless questions of when things will feel clearer and easier again.

I'm so tired of the question of myself, and yet that is the one question I can't escape. Nature helps a great deal in those moments for it's easier to ground myself when I'm in nature, and I allow myself to soak in, observe her sensory imagery, and quiet my mind.

I realize once again I'm breaking away from an old version of self, and it's as shattering now as it was the first time.

When I can't spirit away my messy shambles, and I need to just be in my humanness, I revisit the lessons of my younger self quite a bit. She learned much about being a true human, how grief and joy are intertwined, and that the purpose of this life is to become who we're meant to be.

Sometimes I pretend we're sitting down for a cup of tea together. I picture me as my 2015ish self, who had been through several cracking opens, and who had restitched her pieces into a very compassionate, authentic being.

She (I) was well fomented at that time. After several years of rapid-fire change, Life gifted me with a period of love, serenity and calm. I had a firm sense of who I was, a stable ground to stand on, and I was in my personal power and embodying the energy of love.

In my mind, she and I are having tea. I tell her how hard everything has been, how dissolved I've felt, how confusing and under construction life is. With a twinkle in her eye, she uncrosses her legs, plants her feet on the ground, and leans in on a pair of those bright high heels I always used to wear. Then in a calm reassuring voice, she says —

Oh honey, I'm so proud of you. Congratulations on trusting the trail of becoming a true human. You're doing beautifully. Keep going; I know whatever is waiting for you is going to be worth it.

98

High Priestess

My dear woman,
not all castles
are created equal —
not all foundations
built to outlast,
withstand,
endure
a legacy of light.

And you
dear one,
are building something
meant to ignite
and hold a candle
in the darkest
of nights.

Your mystic heart,
and priestess path
have taken you
to love's great vast —

Your steps of grace,
unwavering faith,
have instilled in you
gifts that outlast.

So, breathe
my dear one,
breathe.
and trust the voice
of your soul's
wise-ease:

All things will happen
as they're meant —
according to
Love's Time.

99

THE FIRE WITHIN

S omewhere back around the end of July, when I realized the only reason I was going to make rent was due to the birthday money my parents gave me, and the beginning of August, when my husband got severely ill and ended up in the hospital for four days, I had a realization I didn't particularly like:

I realized I was being cracked open by the universe again. Circumstances coalesced to bust my seams, my previous version of self-spilling out in disheveled waves of uncertainty and a sense of confusion and ineptitude.

I've cried in public more times than I wanted to count. Yelled at the angels in my car, screaming about how hard it's been to find my footing and purpose on this island. Battled emotions of despair and desolation, all while trying to stay on track.

If there is an invisible world inside each of us, a world that we access through feelings, intuition, and dropping into our heart-still space, then I began to realize my universe within was going through another quaking and shaking.

The terrain of my soul was once again shifting.

I wish I could say I willingly surrendered into the arms of the universe with perfect trust and belief, but my tempestuous heart has always been more fire than water, and I raged and ached along the way, wondering how much more my heart could take.

Seems like ever since we lost Brent life has been nothing but change, release, and learning to find center when the pieces of life tumble apart.

I remember, with sardonic grief, how back in late May, I'd been working with a fellow intuitive, and I asked some version of my standard question, "What's next for me on my soul path?" Her answer stuck, because of its resonance and clarity:

"The universe is inviting you to go even deeper into your relationship with it. It wants to reveal itself to you in greater ways and offer

you a profound and deep learning. All you have to do is say yes, jump in and be taken for a ride."

I said *yes* in my heart in the days to come.

I said *yes*, because who wouldn't want to dive deeper into the fabric of love and better understand the divine mysteries?

I said *yes*, because I've not turned the universe down yet when I've been invited to go deeper.

I said *yes*, because I don't know how to say no to my heart and being drawn inwards and upwards by the intelligence of the divine; it's who I am, it's why I'm here, it's what drives my purpose.

I said *yes* making the fundamentally mistaken assumption I have made every time the universe takes me on another rite of passage. The assumption being: *I always expect the journey to look differently (i.e. easier, better, and more glamorous) than it does.*

I expect new insights to come through while taking contemplative walks in nature or have brilliant epiphanies during my journal time. I expect something magical to just appear, which lends itself to spiritual revelation and growth. I suppose I expect it to happen without working for it, and I always forget we have to descend to ascend if we truly want soul transformation.

Diving into our wreckage is how we find our diamonds of love and hope. Going through dark nights of the soul unveils the stickiest aspects of our humanity, so we can better reveal the light within.

The light is always within when we can stay present with our suffering, drop into our heart and muster up a way to shine a little love into the mess: a pinprick of light and hope, which reminds us the eternal truth of our soul is so much more than the temporary truth of our pain.

The light teaches us that learning to come back to a space of love inside of ourselves is exactly why we are here. We find love only to lose it again and again; we lose love only to find it again and again.

The light teaches we cannot be separated from love. Ever. The divine light lives inside of us; separation is an illusion; love is our truth.

We're not doing anything wrong when we forget this truth, it's just part of the human experience, so new growth can happen every time we return to the truth. Every time we find a way to bring in more light and more love into our space of self, we allow our hearts to hold more space for light and love.

Every time we choose to find a way to shine our heart light, it gets a little brighter, our energy field grows, and we become more powerful in our capacity to anchor space for love.

As late August passes into late September, humid days of jungle green and Kauai's keen scent of ocean and mystery blend and bend into one another, while I contemplate matters of love and the heart.

I press my hand to mine often. Feeling where it's blocked, feeling where it's cracked. I have grief over the difficulties and disillusionment I've experienced on this island, and I ask Archangel Raphael to help me heal my heart. Archangel Ariel helps me understand sometimes the heart is like a hermit crab, who needs to go inside of its shell to protect its boundaries and space of self. She reminds me the heart will always seek out greater expansion after a necessary contraction.

I journal, meditate, pray, and show up in my outer world as I can, while I continue to dig deeper inside, following my red strings of truth to new spaces of depth and knowledge. I ponder the idea the entire universe is encoded in the heart. Perhaps the divine blueprint we are looking for is inside of ourselves, and we become our own cartographers as we learn to listen, perceive, and read our map.

Perhaps this is the true intelligence of the heart: *Not only does the heart have the capacity to love, but it can lead us back to the truth of ourselves over and over again.*

I had intended for 2019 to look so very different — I rocketed into the year like a burning flame, ready to take my place on the stage of life and step into a leadership position. Instead, I have gone underground into the marshes of Yoda's Dagaba system. I am Luke Skywalker facing my own darkness and nature of self in the swamps.

It's in the swamps I find my light. Not on the mountaintop. Not under clear skies. Not when everything is going breezy, and I'm congratulating myself on my terrific success. I certainly don't find it in my old, intact version of self.

It is the dank swamps, where I'm forced to return and nourish my heart in new ways which make me realize this love I'm feeling inside; this universe of inner wisdom (which only gets deeper every time we attend and nourish it); this love I am feeling in all my broken, inept mess; this gracious love, which allows me to return to myself judgment and condemnation free (because even when I forget myself, the Love knows I am never separate from its whole):

This love is the true fire within.

100

Manifesto of Belief

I know it's been tangled and hard, but my dear girl, let me tell you what you're going to do — you're going to trust yourself. Against the odds. Against what lays unseen.

You're going to trust yourself beyond numbers on paper and the questions which sit unanswered in your heart.

You're going to trust yourself in the debris. In the breaking. In your grief. In the deconstruction of self and the unknown pieces of psyche's submergence.

You're going to trust yourself and hold your own hand through your fall from who you once were.

You're going to forget about the instant success-ers and mind over matter manifest-ers and "positive vibes only" tribes, which disconnect you from the most integral pieces of yourself: the darkness within, which exists to guide you through the tunnels in life where the soul goes quiet as it prepares for rebirth.

You're going to trust yourself when it looks like everybody else is winning and you're losing.

You're going to trust some days your wins will be getting out of bed and moving forwards.

Maybe your purpose here is to be the most human you can possibly be. To embody every inch of your humanity and shine with your faith that our inherent divinity still exists within this human space.

You're going to trust that human space. Trust the trail of being a true human. Trust the trail of real in all its gritty splendor and glossy mess.

You're going to trust the brokenness, your chipped parts and all the times you strive and fail. You're going to trust failure is success in its own form and the divine is moving your experiences together and revealing the bigger picture of you in its own time.

You're going to trust your own drunken imperfections and tipsy discombobulations and intoxicated tribulations — and you're going to become an expert on emotional reincarnation.

For you will resurrect and rebirth and reinvent yourself over and over again. So, you're going to trust your feelings, and see they are all part of the same tangled ball of red yarn leading you deeper into yourself. Deeper into your heart. Deeper into love. Deeper into the divine.

Deeper into the truth that is you.

Sky Above Me

Light within me.
Light below me.
Light around me.
Light above me.

So, shall I be.

101

My Magic

I like to think I have many forms of magic: My heart's ability to feel, heal, tunnel deep, fall upwards, love, mend and bend.

My soul's well-trained ear, who listens to the in-betweens and hears the speak of angelic sings.

My relationship with the natural world, who constantly teaches me the biggest miracles are hidden before our eyes, so we need to take the shells off and learn to see with a child's mind.

But my words are their own form of magic. Writing transmutes experiences into alchemical gold. Diving into feelings creates new elements and compounds of sea-salt and soul-gold.

We become the mystic shaman when we write. Weaving stories out of the dreams of our lives. Creating our own myths and mysteries, unearthing new prophecies where we weave the elements of our histories — to script a new future to navigate by.

Sunshine daffodil joy. Caramel autumn bittersweet. Ocean grief blues. Icy white truths: *words are the alchemists who emotionally evoke and transmute.*

When I write, I go into my spirit's apothecary shop, where I can explore, mix, essence and brew. A pinch of this, a dab or two. I string words like kite tails from alphabet soup. Healing and feeling and sealing anew; transcribing this life from observer's view:

Rebirthing, reforming, rewriting the story from a lens drenched in love.

102

Two Poems from Glass Beach

i.

blue cobalt music
glass brine salt
a tired heart
& all my fault —

lines chip and crack
on ocean's west shore;
I don't know myself,
where I belong
anymore.

except by the sea...
(who returns me
to me)
...a maritime anchor
in deepest of need

I seek my
completion
on grains of
her glass;
my waters are endless

my soul-well too vast
to
fully
grasp.

ii.

Wave in the sun child.
Wave in the sun.
Wave by the surf and be one.

Return to the core of who you are,
your palm-lines and star-signs
hold clues to your farthest
depths and intuitive seas;
it's okay to trust in the things you can't see.

Yet feel in your heart and your stirring of soul
— don't seek for your truth among those who don't know
how to follow the strings of spirit's moon-speak
and dance with the cosmos in unspoken beat —
defying what cannot be grasped 'cept by heart
the doorway that opens the truth of your art.

(If you've happened to lose where your true art starts,
all you need know is your art is your heart
so, follow its flows and trust — see where it leads…
there you shall unlock your truth's mysteries.)

Wave in the sun child.
Wave in the sun.
Wave by the surf and be one.

103

THE GOLDEN CORD

I have a message for you of clarity. I, Gabriel, who helps you find inspired voice.

Picture a golden cord connecting you from throat to solar plexus to your root chakra. Picture this thread helping align all parts of you with your truth.

You are divine. You are supported. You are creative. You are loved.

Allow the cord to dissolve away any doubt or confusion, any fear of judgment. Let it fill you with light. Breathe in my light. Open your throat and breath in my light.

Now you are ready to speak greater truth. Know you are ready to speak greater truth.

Allow yourself space to breathe your truth. Your truth is love. Find as many ways to speak love as you can in all things.

Create with the clarity you are awakening greater love in others. Create to be an activator of love. Pour this intent into all that you do and see how the truth springs free with ease and joy.

104

WILD HORSES

*I*t was early in the morning on September 19th, 2019, the day right after Saturn left retrograde. I had read this would create a big shift with a lot of fresh energy being freed up.

Astrologically, Saturn represents where we feel restricted and limited. It's been camping out in the house of Capricorn (which represents traditional structures and hard work) for a while now. What makes this interesting, is that Saturn has been hanging with the karmic south node (which represents what we're releasing and letting go of in this lifetime), along with Pluto (which represents what we're evolving into).

This particular transit has been going on throughout 2019 and will culminate with a final eclipse on December 26, 2019. On a global scale, we are seeing old structures and traditions being challenged as new ways of being, which feel more harmonious, cooperative, and collective, emerge.

On a personal level, these transits are happening in a very auspicious place on my star chart. For simplicity, I'll simply say: *Even the cosmos seems to be mirroring the themes of my life.*

I've been so wrapped up in my emotional and occupational mire that I didn't think too much of the date until 2:22 am, when I suddenly woke and sat straight up in bed with one thought running through my mind, "What if you let yourself out of the gate?"

Let me back up and explain:

There has been a reoccurring image running through my mind for the last year. I've had a felt sense of being trapped and held back. This sensation always comes with the intuitive image of a racehorse, chomping at the bit, ready to let loose on the track, stuck in a cage, behind her gate.

For whatever reason, it's just not her time to race. She watches all the other horses run around the track in freedom, and she's hungry for her shot. She's ready to be unleashed.

This whole past year, I've been waiting for somebody, something, someone to come unleash me. Then at 2:22 am, my dream-speak wakes me and bids me out of bed with this sudden turn of perspective.

I get up and go into my office, settle on my meditation pillows as I light a candle, grab my journal. I spend time writing, contemplating and intuiting what it would look like to let myself out of the gate, and I begin to feel something weighty start to shift inside my chest.

Sometimes spirit is subtle, but there are times where the signs and synchronicities light up like flashing neon arrows. I find that over the course of the next three nights I consistently wake up at 2:22 am with the compulsion to get up, return to my meditation space, and listen to my heart, intuition and spiritual connection.

New ideas begin to flow in. Out of the box. Untried ideas. New thoughts come through on how to pull my platform together in more effective ways, so all the pieces are gathered under a greater whole.

I realize I've been creating all these separate pieces from an intuitive, organic space, but I've lacked the greater vision of how they all work together and what my mission and purpose is truly about.

I realize everything I create teaches an aspect of how to trust and heed our heart and intuitive self, and I make a list of the different ways I teach these things: *Honoring our emotions. Listening to our hearts. Living close to nature and cultivating creativity. Expanding our minds and opening our consciousness.*

I will later find a note in my journal that says: "When we do these things, we engage with our intuitive self and organically tap into our voice of soul."

This represents a tipping point for my business: I decide to view, "Dr. BethAnne K.W." as a company, and I view myself as the brand ambassador and CEO of my company. Meager though my company is, I start to think more strategically and intelligently about what I'm trying to build.

In days to come, I'll find I've stopped feeling threatened and intimidated by the idea of promoting myself and begin to feel more excited about the idea of confidently sharing my work.

On one of my 2:22 a.m. epiphany nights, I feel called to send the energy of love to my business, because I realize the soul of my business feels broken and heavy. I'm initially resistant that this is the cure I'm being offered by spirit; I feel like my business needs lots of things — fresh energy, monetary investment, greater resources — and I don't understand what good sending it love will do.

However, the urge is so insistent I heed it, and I begin to picture the energy of love radiating to "Dr. BethAnne K.W." Vitalizing blues to cleanse and renew. Bold reds to empower and lead. Creamy pinks to heal and mend.

It is in this process that I realize Love doesn't need me to tell it what to do for my business. The energy of Love is intelligent enough to help repair my business in its own divine way. This knowledge is a rare canary diamond, and it deepens my understanding of how the intelligence of love works.

Things begin to shift after this. It's not all immediate. I have a lot of work to do, and I realize I need to get comfortable living outside of my comfort zone.

I have, however, begun to see the bigger path and a greater picture of myself. I've been praying for a vision, a bird's eye view, to understand the greater whole of my calling and what I'm trying to create. Just when I felt like giving up, I've been given it.

I am fighting for myself. Fighting for my dreams. Fighting for love and for my soul calling. I am taking greater responsibility and realizing I am not entitled to have things come easily or show up on my doorstep — I will earn my passage and my privilege to be a dream-bearer and change-maker. I am releasing old ideals and surrendering the fantasy of how I thought my dreams would look — so I can actualize my dreams in real ways. There is grief in the process, and yet there is also new life being born.

I don't know where this is going, I don't know how it will crystallize, but this is the moment that marks the change when I began to truly hold onto my greater vision: *to be a global transformational author, speaker, and teacher who holds space for the light and awakens the light in others with my words and work.*

I feel so far away from the success of that, yet I begin to strive to embody the energy now. As if it already happened. I begin to realize it's no longer a matter of if, but when, and I am tasked to take what tangible steps I can. When doubt creeps in, I will be guided to return to the heart of my vision, again and again, understanding the *how* of it might change, but the core of it will not.

I realize I was always meant to have a clearer knowing when the time was right. My path wasn't hidden from me out of punishment or abandonment, but to shape me into a woman who could truly hold the space for her bold vision and be fearless enough to get out of her own way and grow it.

I begin to realize something in the days to come: my sense of being a trapped racehorse is gone, and it's not because I'm out on the track with the other horses running around in circles.

I am galloping across new fields into new horizons. Blazing my trail in my own way. Carving out the path with each stride and step. The terrain is more rugged here, purer, untouched, closer to the heart of the earth. I know now, the image I once had of being locked behind the gate was entirely wrong: I never was meant to be somebody's racehorse.

I am an untamed thing running wild and free.

105

Slowly Rising

It's slowly waking up.
This vision inside born
through the fires of
grief's winter ice.

Pushing up and against
a still thawing ground,
growing, yet waiting,
with patience for time.

Prepared to break through
and break out when right,
when the voice within
my heart-still space guides —

Beloved, now is your time
to arise.

106

WILD AND WISE

*I*t can be a hard truth to surrender into: Life is bigger than us and we're asked to yield to it often.

Yet there's grace in this truth as well. Grace in yielding and realizing we're not in control and not in charge.

There's also grace in grief. In allowing it to be a storm, which sweeps through us and helps, potentially, press reset.

Grief awakens and rearranges. It's a difficult process, yet it can also be beautiful when we intuitively follow grief's flows and discover they lead back to love.

And Love is wild and wise.

Love knows how to instinctually, inventively, and ingenuously heal the wounds within, fill our cracks with liquid gold, and help us become our true selves.

We don't have to try so hard to figure out how to mend, we just have to surrender to love's wisdom and know all things repair, renew and return to light in their own time.

107

ANGEL MESSAGES ON A TUESDAY MORN

*D*o not get lost in the day to day. You must learn to see flow and beauty where others might see work and ordinary. Try and see all of it as creation and what you are creating, and it will make your human life shine with divine luster.

Use the opportunities you have in your day to breathe, to think, to feel, to pause, to pray. Let your life be a living prayer, let the steps you take be thoughtful, mindful and purposed to the cause of Love.

Do not worry about doing this perfectly, do not worry at all. Instead, use these words as a compass to return to when you feel lost. *How can you be more purposeful? How can you be more intentional? How can you be more appreciative of your human moments? How can you bring your heart into the pieces of your day?*

Look for the ways you can bring your heart into the pieces of your days. In as many ways as you can. Do this, and you begin to create love wherever you go. Do this and you learn to flow from the heart, to follow its lead, to heed its natural intelligence. Do this and you will truly bestow upon others as you would desire bestowed upon you.

This is how you create in your world. This is how you bring good things into you: by doing good things for others. By loving others. By allowing that energy to flow back into you.

We are not talking about the kind of love where you don't feel you deserve receiving love in equal accord. That is obligation. This is not that kind of equation. No, we are talking about giving love from generosity of spirit, knowing you are deserving of love being poured back into you. This is an important part of the equation, so you learn to care for yourself and respect your own worth.

Give with an open heart when you feel called to give and know you deserve to receive in abundance. Get ready to receive in abundance. For that is an important part of love too.

Walk the beauty way in truth. There are many who've walked that path before you. Look to them, call on them, know you are surrounded by clouds of ancestors who support you in this work.

Be at peace in the flow. Be at peace in the flow and know all things are working together in accordance with the divine flow. Trust your heart. Trust your journey. Trust your SELF. Remember, you can always trust yourselves.

108

Tunneling into Trust

"You can always trust yourself."
That's what the angels said, and it pierces me.

I sit with this wisdom and take it deep into my heart, deep into my core as I allow the words to truly sink into me. Trust is an ongoing theme in my life, yet these words strike a chord in a new, unplayed way.

The angels have such confidence in us, maybe they truly do see what we can't often see in our own selves: our innate ability to shine and thrive.

I know trust isn't a one-time linear deal, it is a continuous surrender, and I have been trying to surrender. Yet I know I'm still hanging on trying to control how I think things should look, as if I don't trust myself enough to be in an unknown space and figure it out.

These words place another seed within, and I plant it in my heart as I think about what would it be like to truly trust myself?

What would it be like to trust my lonely?

What would it be like to trust every experience I've had of love?

What would it be like to trust that I've been on the right path all along, and any unknowing was simply there as a tool to lead me into deeper knowing?

What would it be like to trust my story, because when we trust our stories, we are more fully able to own our stories?

What would it be like to trust my emotional experience of self?

My psychological experience of self?

My physical experience of self?

My mental, experiential, and intuitive experience of self?

The angel's words on trust are so simple, and yet they bring revolution to my psyche, and my intuition guides me to begin working with trust in a new way.

I begin saying out loud as a daily practice: *I trust myself. I trust myself not to know. I trust myself to figure it out. I trust my emotional experience of self. I trust my heart to love as it loves. I trust my heart to heal as it heals. I trust myself to grow in my own way in my own time.*

On and on I go, finding ways to affirm trust in almost all aspects of my being. It is Libra season, the element is air, and air represents new thoughts, new ideas, and new perspectives. Our minds can be powerful tools that either support our growth, allowing us to choose higher perspective more rooted in truth, or hinder our growth by refusing to release toxic ways of thinking.

I choose to release. I choose new perspective. I choose to rewire my neural networks. I choose more constructive ways of thinking. I choose self-honoring ways of thinking, which encompass both my human and spiritual natures. I choose to evolve past old patterns of fear. I choose deeper truth.

I choose to trust myself.

109

Balsamic Moon

*M*isty green, yellowing banana leaves, fairy rings sing on the breeze. There is beauty in such tiny things as October streams with waning moon and changeful breeze.

Truth may not always feel kind, but I'm learning it will always free. Self-love begins with learning to listen to the heart and find ways to honor my needs. Fuzzy socks and old soft tees ground thoughtful nights into candlelit cozy.

Transformation's crystal droplet sways the window of my soul. I find myself metamorphosing into new form, though I can still feel the dense coat of my old. Letting go happens in spirals, squiggles and grace notes —

And small puffs of wind and tiny insights that string together like Christmas lights illuminating the way within. Somewhere between then and now, I keep finding my way back again: into my heart-still space where truth's release cleans the wound and heals the mend.

Receptive. Reflective. Selective. Protective: My seed-dreams require boundaries and care, so they have space to spring into life. Moon's face remains my forever friend, who helps origin a new phase and new side. Veracity's capacity to transfigure reaches wide:

Love's voice flows through cross purple seas: *Investing in maintaining a smaller version of self will only prolong your rise.*

110

Love Knows Us

*T*iming is perhaps one of the hardest things to trust and allow when we feel growth inside of ourselves and want to make something happen in our lives.

Perhaps it is a rite of passage on the spiritual path where we must learn to yield to the divine and trust all things will come to be in their own time. Perhaps this is a process we go through again and again, as we learn and explore what the word surrender truly means.

Maybe this is like playing with a pair of the brightly woven finger cuffs we played with back in childhood: the harder we effort and try and pull our fingers out, the more stuck we become.

It is only in becoming the wisdom of the 8 of Swords — in realizing the more we struggle, the more we ensnare ourselves in the trap — we can begin to ease and relax, to loosen our grip, and allow ourselves to find another way through. Trusting we will be guided, so we can see a better way.

We must learn to see the better way in our lives. The paradigm is shifting, and the time is over for playing by the book, reacting out of fear of what may happen, and efforting away because we feel we must.

The world is evolving in such a way that each of us is being ushered into a deeper relationship with the divine. One where we take a bigger sense of responsibility for being a co-creator of our lives, when we realize: Life isn't happening to us. We are happening with Life.

It's a process where we are evolving together, and what beautiful news this is:

Love wants to dance with us.

To create with us.

To write new pages with us.

To bid us leave the rigidity of old books behind and learn to live by the book of the heart.

This is a book whose pages are being written every time we go inside and listen to our heart's wisdom, and every time we find a way to return to love. Knowing that Love's timing isn't necessarily the same timing our minds would like, but it will be better than anything we could have imagined.

This is what we're being taught to trust.

This is what I'm being taught to trust in this vulnerable time of need, grief, confusion, and new vision in my life: *to release the old paradigm of the struggle.*

It is a struggle we create every time we default to the space of needing to know how it will turn out.

We already know how it will turn out. We've been told in multiple scriptures in multiple forms throughout history, by multiple trusted teachers, visionaries, and channels of higher power — *it is all working towards the higher cause of love and we are seen, held and loved in the process, so it also works together for our higher cause.*

Can you imagine what would happen if we actually trusted *that?*

Then the unknown isn't fearful, because it's actually the known. The known of love. The known of who we are when we live in love. Even if we can't see our way through the immediate path in front of us, we've already been given a picture of the greater path:

Love knows us. Love we know. It is through this knowledge we will always find the way home to our soul.

111

The Illusion

*"Three things cannot be long hidden: the sun,
the moon, and the truth."*

— BUDDHA

*T*here is a card in one of my oracle decks called *Discernment*. I started pulling it regularly back in the summer, and the meaning is about seeing something through the eyes of truth. Seeing with wisdom and clarity. Seeing something for what it really is, instead of how we think it is.

I work with different decks regularly in my intuitive practice, so when the same card keeps popping up, or the same message from different sources, I pay attention.

There is also a card in the tarot called *The 7 of Swords*. It represents seeing through illusions and sometimes indicates someone is being deceptive in your life and not telling the truth.

Another card in the tarot, *The Moon*, echoes this sentiment, encouraging us to delve below the surface of things and realize all is not as it appears to be. *The Moon* asks us to consider the questions: *What is not being illuminated in our lives and where is the illusion?*

What is important to note about all of these cards is that in almost every reading I've done since my birthday back in July, they've been popping up over and over again. The themes of truth, illumination, deception, and discernment are rife in my life at this time.

When I was younger, even just a few years back, these kinds of cards made me nervous. *Oh no! What am I not seeing? Is somebody tricking me?*

I interpreted them as if they indicated somebody in my life was lying to me or not being honest. I would feel like I was doing something wrong, wondering what I was missing in a situation or if I was foolishly allowing the wool to be pulled over my eyes.

It's a fear-based interpretation. Rooted in the idea that I can't trust myself to see with clarity. Or trust that whatever truths I need to know will unveil and reveal in time.

I've grown since then. Kauai has forced me to face my fears and root so firmly in the light and knowledge of myself, I now know how to interpret these cards without fear. I understand the message spirit is trying to bring through: *The illusion and deception aren't what's going on outside of you, it's what's going on inside of you.*

I've been lying to myself.

I lie to myself every time I tell myself I'm not good enough.

I lie to myself every time I believe my voice doesn't matter.

I lie to myself every time I look at my current circumstances and mistake them for my soul's truth.

The deception lays inside of myself when I don't recognize my true worth.

(The deception lays inside all of us when we don't recognize our true worth).

Working with the energy of trust is changing me. Healing my self-trust wound is helping me see that my deepest illusion is judging my success and value based on the circumstantial evidence of my life right now.

Every time I send myself the message that I can't trust myself to know myself and sense my path and that I can't trust my relationship with spirit and the visions I've been given for my life, I am really telling myself that I can't trust my soul's unfolding process.

This goes against everything I teach and claim to be.

I decide to take this insight as an opportunity for deeper healing, when I'm in my heart-still space and dialed into the energy of love. I picture the part of myself who has struggled to feel seen, heard and valued, and I send her love.

Radiant pink. Joyful yellow. The mantle of piercing violet blue truth.

I picture the younger me who saw her value tied to her profession as a psychologist, I used to wonder if I'd still matter to people as much if I wasn't always helping them, holding space for them, or being what I believed they needed me to be for them.

I send her love too, and I send her the wisdom that the matter of 'mattering' far supersedes our utility in our professions.

I think about myself just yesterday: Last night I sat discouraged after another day of creating, sharing, posting, emailing, trying to feel like my work as a spiritual and intuitive teacher is having an impact, and not getting the tangible results I desire.

Yesterday self gets loads of love too; I send streams of turquoise, ruby and lapis her way.

I trust healing is taking place. Because I've learned something about the energy of love this last season: Love's energy is Source energy, God's energy, and the spiritual material of grace that knits this world together.

This divine energy is creative, intuitive, and highly intelligent and will know exactly what to do to heal the broken places I've directed it to.

It will love them and nourish them. It will mend broken seams. It will lift any necessary action steps to the front of my consciousness. So, I don't have to control my own healing process or try so hard to heal: That's Love's job, and I trust it.

I trust I am enough for Love.

I trust I capable of receiving Love.

I trust I deserve to be healed of my illusions, so I can become a greater vessel for Love.

112

SACRED SEERS

I woke up early today, Brent on my mind. Tears intertwined before dawn sang wake and night's stars become superseded by day's light.

Magenta streaked the sky, and a passing thought went by that life can be a terrible beast, but there's splendor too within its lines. Sometimes all it takes is a mindful moment to pull the good back inside; retrieve what's pure and right:

Enfold the daffodils and let them be a balm for hardship and gray-grief. Find the soft music of sunrise and notes of grace within cloud's cream-sheets. Trace the curves of a word until it becomes a raindrop washing our dreams blue-clean.

In those moments we re-collect ourselves and reassemble our pieces into a bigger whole. Remember the light-flow we forget we know. Return to a space where the wild things grow. In those moments we augur, resonate, elevate, and illustrate heart's gold:

It is only in the sacred still we seer our truth of soul.

113

EPITAPH

O ne of my favorite things about being a writer is that you can express whatever thought-streams you want, dipping your pen into whatever heart-depths your currents go.

Sometimes the waters are bright and rainbow; sometimes poetry fill-flowed; and sometimes you get called to dive deep and explore the things and strings which tug most at soul.

Grief is often found in my deep-dive bottomless watery cosmos. Surrounded by a silty sea of love: *for I loved, therefore I grieve, and I grieve because I love.*

Old memories of my brother are always waiting in this tender space. I'm swept back to winter of 2016, and suddenly I'm not three and a half years into my grief journey, but at the origin. Remembering those lonely, still steps when I first learned what it truly meant to carry grief in the way only a sister can.

Grievers know things others do not. Sometimes this sets us apart and this can be hard. But it can be beautiful too if we learn to see the magnitude of our own becoming and our strength. We learn to bear what seemed unbearable, and we learn the gifts of buried light and fierce grace throughout grief's length.

There are times when I don't know if that girl from 2016 will ever fully heal. Then I remember I don't need to: healing will come as it comes, how it comes, where it comes. In accordance with its own intuitive wisdom.

And surely to hurt because I still love him so much is its own alchemy of mystical healing.

In the meantime, words are the doorways that travel me through loss's strange waves. Offering medicinal balm and mugs of love to others along the way. Creating quantum leaps in labyrinth's grief, when my tears have run astray...

His epitaph became my heart's lithograph: permanently engraved with the words of a sister's love.

114

I and Sam, Part 1
(written October 2016)

*Y*esterday was a day for the mountains.

October came fast to Alaska, it's the end of fall here, not the height. Especially up in the mountains where the winds and rains have already swept on through and knocked the bulk of leaves off the trees, turning the ground from the brilliant reds, marigolds and green of September to russets and chestnuts and fawn.

I head up into the hills with my old dog, Sam. He's a senior rescue, 13 pounds of sweetness, and built like a footstool with short stubby legs and a stout body which is capable of slow walks, though not good for climbing. I grab his special front pack and tell him I'm packing him up today. Not only do I want his company, but he loves the outdoors. He just can't get all the way up the mountain without an assist, so today I assist.

It's slower to get to the top with Sam. He does a little on his own before he turns around and starts heading back down the trail after realizing it's much easier to go down than it is to come up. After retrieving him, I stick him in his pouch and carry him up through henna brush and tan tundra.

The top is always worth the effort. I can see Anchorage, the Inlet, Ship Creek Valley, South Fork Valley and how everything hooks up and is connected by the miles and miles of mountains and water around here. The wind is whipping, and the sun is dancing in and out of thick heather clouds, and Sam is happily trotting along beside me, now that the hardest part is over.

There is not another soul around. Just Sam and I, I and Sam. We gaze out at long stretches of ridgelines and peaks, with views of blue and brown and turn of season. I pick a point, already sprinkled with a smattering of snow, well across the ridge and head in that direction. I have no agenda, just time, my thoughts, the mountains, and Sam.

I think about my younger days, deeply transformative years when I was always losing myself in the mountains to go find myself. This land carried me through a deconstruction and reconstruction of self, eight years back, and I owe her a debt of gratitude for being there to support and carry me during a time when I was learning to support and carry myself.

The mountains were my container. Letting me come and go as I pleased. Holding and storing and allowing me to leave pieces of myself all over her craggy terrain. Keeping them safe in the depths of her wild heart until I was ready to retrieve my pieces, weep and love and break and examine and cry over them, then find a way to integrate them into the depths of my own wild heart.

I consider how today is not like those younger days. I have no pieces to leave in these hills. Nothing to lose or shed, other than a bit of the stress that has accumulated these past weeks. I am full and whole, and I know:

I know who I am.

I know where I'm going.

I know that it's okay not to know.

The girl from my yesterdays, she didn't know those things. Today she does. She's tucked deep inside of me, part of my past, part of my present, part of my whole.

I pay homage to her by deciding to go long — that's the sort of thing she would have done, staying up there for hours among the ridges — so instead of turning back, I press on further. Let the wind whip my skin. Be in the moment. Smile at my white companion who is doggedly making his way along the ridges, having the time of his life.

I'll miss you, I say out loud to the Land, as I think about our upcoming move and how different the terrain will be in Kauai. She answers back, reminding me though the terrain will change, she is still the same Earth in the green of Hawaii that supports my steps on these October hills today.

I am Everywhere. I am All. She says.

Yes. I think. *She is.*

It will be different there, but the land, the water, the jungle, and the mountains have new things to teach me. Unlike these mountains, which helped contain my younger self's fragmented identity, I'm not going to Kauai to retrieve my pieces of identity and find out who I am. I'm going there to retrieve something needed for my soul.

We remain up there for three hours Sam and I, I and Sam. Exploring, climbing, sitting on the rocks and watching the valleys below. Sometimes Sam walks, sometimes he gets carried. He looks so happy, and I think about how beautiful it is to be with this little being, on this day, in the spotless grace of this place.

As the evening gets closer it's time to drop down. The sun has been covered by great swaths of gray that warn rain is coming in the night. We slide a little on the slick trail and shiver as the winds begin to lash out. The downhill is all mud and stream and auburn and birch, and I smile with bittersweet remembrance of September's crush of emerald and ruby and blond.

It is October. Winter will soon be coming. The leaves are dropping with a pristine courage I envy, for they know when to let go. The land is becoming sleepier preparing itself for November decay. The trees keep reaching on up, reminding us to always move towards the light. The sky is deepening in fond nuance of soft wheat and murky heliotrope and velvet rose. I am Full, and I am Whole, and I Know. I am Everywhere, and I am All.

I am grateful for this gift of day: Sam and I, I and Sam.

115

I and Sam, Part 2
(written October 2019)

I sense Sam often.

I carry him with me now, just as I carry Brent. I know he's out there in spirit, but there's a love I've tucked inside that represents his essence. Our essence. He goes up the mountain with me today, in my heart and in spirit.

It's late Fall in the island's gentle seasonal way. The guava berries have ripened and mostly dropped. Leaves on the jungle trees yellow, preparing to shed so new green can grow. The sun was a tangerine crest this morning. The sky sliding doors of light silver, bold blue, and thoughtful gray.

I sense Sam often.

I miss him and it comforts me, even as it sometimes saddens me, to think of his soft silky fur and sweet disposition.

He will always represent our first year on the island, and for that I am grateful, He is inextricably bound up in my story and journey on Kauai. Sam traveled with us to this island, and he watched over us our first tangled, messy year of strife, life and transformation.

I sense Sam often.

Even as life has gone on and grown itself around the parts he once occupied.

Though whenever *Rambling Rose* comes on, we stop and dance like Sam in honor of Sam. He had this groovy way of trailing along like there was all the time in the world.

So, we do the Sam walk, and we dance in memory, and we keep healing the hole in our hearts left by Sam.

I sense Sam often.

I read the words in an old essay I wrote back in fall of 2016 about Sam. I was so certain then of my path and decision to move to the island. I had my own brand of wisdom back then, hard-earned and reflective of my life experiences. I knew myself well, and I believed I was moving here to become my soulful self.

I didn't realize that to become my soulful self, I would need to deconstruct my identity and previous version of self. I've wondered, if somebody told me how difficult life would be on the island, if I would have still said yes and found the courage to leap. There were moments of darkness last summer, so intense, I realized I didn't want to be here anymore.

Despair and desolation reflected shadow aspects of myself, I wasn't aware existed. I remember crawling through the recesses of doubt, uncertainty, fear, and failure wondering if I had made a mistake in coming to Kauai. Sometimes I thought of Sam in those moments and how he always believed in me and saw the best in me. His unconditional love a candle, even when life went dark.

I sense Sam often.

Whereas Brent feels like he's moved farther away, still close by at times, but not like he was when we first lost him; Sam still feels ever present. As if he never really left at all but remained on in our household as our angel dog.

They say those who have cancer are closer to God. They also say dogs come into this world already knowing unconditional love, so they don't need to be here as long as we do. I figure those two things made Sam one powerful ambassador of Love.

Someday I believe he will come back to us. Dogs can return, you know. A dog's spirit has many lives, our beloved childhood pets are frequently the same ones we love now. They don't always come back, but some of them do.

I believe Sam may.

An image of a wriggly, mop-like dog entered into my stream of consciousness a couple of months back. A premonition of what may come. I keep seeing myself holding this floppy pup, who I've not met and have no knowledge of. Somehow in my vision, I know Sam has chosen to return to us in new form.

This is why I believe he'll come back.

But not yet, it's not time. For Sam or for us. Sam's busy in his afterlife enjoying joy right now. Joyful is how he feels when I feel him. Like he's exploring and rolling in the energy of joy. No wonder I always see pink roses and yellow daffodils in my mind's eye when I sense him.

I sense Sam often.

I remember all the times I carried him up a mountain. Tucked into his little satchel for most of the way, punctuated with short bursts of hiking he did himself. I knew myself so well then, back in my old Alaska version of self. I did an outstanding job embodying my prior version of self, but that's not who I came to Kauai to be.

Sam taught me transitions can be hard, but they are part of life. We will each die to ourselves and birth ourselves many times over. If we can return to what is most important inside of ourselves, return to the heart and return to the love, this process becomes easier. We'll remember we are never separate from love and love is always waiting for us to return, welcoming us with open arms.

Sam is in my heart-space now. His spirit goes on, yet the love we created and the memory of who he was while he was here on earth as our pup and our friend — the love lives on inside of me. I like to think that love acts as a lighthouse for him, making it easy to guard and guide our family in angel form.

Love acts like a honing signal he can spiritually anchor into, remaining close by. He can find us easily, because there's still so much love.

And I am stronger because of our love: Sam and I, I and Sam.

116

What Loss Has to Teach Us

"In this moment, there is plenty of time.
In this moment, you are precisely as you should be.
In this moment, there is infinite possibility."
— VICTORIA MORAN

W e don't always recognize the sacredness of our life. Tapping into the precious quality of our breaths, the potential we each hold as individuals, and the nature of our own light is something we have to learn. We don't come here knowing it.

That is the heart wisdom we gain along the journey, something we must first experience to truly embrace. Experience is the difference between knowing about something and actually living and embodying something. And we can't fully embody life, if we haven't been through loss.

Loss is our teacher, who heightens our experience of life and creates a greater awareness of how beautiful and finite it is. Loss is the catalyst who can catapult us into a new consciousness. Loss holds the potential for tremendous transformation when we can grab onto the full of its lessons.

There is no greater teacher on Life's brief, glorious wisp than Death.

It is only through knowing finality, that we can see how sacred our wisp of self is, how sacred is the journey, how sacred is the ALL of life. Because we are here — here in the beautiful, difficult, finite, possible space of this place.

It means we have chances. Choices. Possibilities.

What a gift is the light of our own possibility. Inherently holy and hallowed, precious and cherished, prayerful and revered, sublime and divine. What a privilege to be present to embrace the opportunities that are our lives.

Our deepest darks are often found in the loss of something or someone, which was sacred, precious, and dear to us. Our brightest light can be found when we grapple with the terms of life — that all things must end so they can come around in new form. When we grapple with death, we gradually learn to come to terms with cessation, opening ourselves up to the truth of our own being in ways we were unable to previously realize.

We hold the potential to find new openings when life hands us a close. An opening, which can help us realize how sacred everything is. From the most heightened to the most mundane, from the beautiful to the awful, from the sorrow to the joy.

It can all become a chance to embody each moment we are given as best we can.

To be full in our grief. To be full in our love. To own and stretch and delve into whatever emotional experience we have on each given day. To embrace the presence of a moment, whether we like the moment or not. To live more courageously, honestly, boldly. To simply sit still and belong to this world.

To see the sacred in the whole of our lives.

We were never promised life would look a certain way. We were only promised a chance to make the most of what comes our way. Promised our own spark of self. Promised soul growth. Promised a chance at humanity and a chance for the evolution of our hearts. Promised opportunities to learn about love in all its diverse forms.

As long as we are here, we have the gift of possibility. The gift of growth. The gift of hope. The gift of falling deeper into Love. The gift of reaching and lengthening and evolving into bigger, more nuanced beings. The gift of hurting when we pain. Celebrating when we joy. The gift of carrying our losses in our hearts and letting those losses strengthen us in love and affirmation of our own humanity.

The gift of continuing to strive to embody the peace, change, and grace we so wish to see in the hallowed halls of these precious, sacred days.

117

BROKEN AND WHOLE

M aybe we move through life both broken and whole. Where it's not an either or but a symbiotic relationship; each time we find a break within our self, we are afforded the opportunity to heal it a little more, moving us into greater wholeness.

I often think about how broken I've felt on this island. How many places I've cried, shook, disorganized, and felt an aching vulnerability of not knowing who I am. Even as all my wounds of self, gifted me with new space to transcend older versions of BethAnne and become a more authentic, bigger being.

Perhaps I'm just in a space where I'm broken right now, and I need to get used to it. I said to a soul sister the other day, *"Maybe Kauai is where I get to be messy, vulnerable and real."*

"And really, why would you want to be any other way?" She said, with the way she has of speaking searing truth in the most unexpected moments.

I think about this in the days to come and sit with the question in my heart: *Why would we want to be any other way?*

Broken is what it is to be a true human, Whole is what it means to be innately divine. When we realize we are always slightly broken in our humanity, we realize we can never be truly broke. Instead, we learn to see our breaks as the place where we can receive, unveil, and reveal the true light within. The light of our soul.

Being broken is how we also know ourselves whole.

We become chiseled and hollowed out by life's hardships, which carry the potential to move us into a transformative space of mending our wounds with perspective, prayer, self-expression, and love.

Every time we allow another old fragment of unhealed self to fall away, we have the opportunity to move from old stories and mistruth (our ego's perception of who we think we should be) into vital, lifegiving truth (our soul's knowledge of who we really are).

We understand our darkness only sharpens a greater understanding of our light, allowing us to become more whole and alive in love.

We become vessels of light when we allow this process to happen. Columns of peace and grace, who can continually hold more space for love to come onto the planet, because we've chosen to make space within by holding space for ourselves. Holding space for our humanness. Our brokenness. Our struggles.

Our wholeness is what allows us to courageously attend our breaks; our brokenness is what makes us whole and brings us closer to the truth of our soul.

118

BIRTHRIGHT OF LIGHT

Listen,
if you will,
to how the sky speaks
grief and love within
the same prescient breath.

How the syntax
of green grass
tip, tap, types out
a message of hope
for the living.

The Delphian stars
guide and divine,
while the kind cows
beseech:
*Learn to lead
with heart's mind.*

For this world is alive
with magical guides,
each of us has
the breath of divine,
we just need choose
to truth, trust, take flight —

Permission and wing
our birthright of light.

119

ARIEL & JOPHIEL'S LUMINATIONS

*I*t starts in the heart and flows from there. The heart is the center of the flower and as it opens it sends information to all other parts of the flower.

The heart is the passageway everything must go through to fully synthesize and integrate.

Tend to your hearts and all will be well. They will lead you home into the promised land, into the heaven inside of you, residing in your core.

Tend to your heart like you tend to the earth — with wisdom, gratitude and reverence. Tend to your heart like you thank the earth for supporting, uplifting and nourishing you. Embrace your heart like you embrace the earth — with gratitude that it is all part of the sacred creation of soul.

Your heart is where your wealth resides, your heart is where your riches reside. Your heart is where new earth resides.

Your soul is a mighty diamond. When you return to it through your heart, you polish its facets and keep shining it.

Each of you has so much light residing within. Every time you polish the mirror, the lens through which you view yourself, aim to uncloud it a little more, then a little more, so you can keep on seeing your divinity. Your starlit nature. Your true shine.

Look to the stars as wise teachers on this. They shine on their own accord without fear or care for how others are shining. So too, must you.

Polish your diamonds, uncloud the mirror, return to the heart, and keep feeling and filling your light.

Blessed be all divinity. Each of you is so very loved.

120

The Lady in Red

*I*t begins with a woman in a scarlet cape, walking through the snow. *Your heart is trying to free itself in bigger ways,* comes through on the wind, as a dove white owl flies nearby.

The ground lays frozen, covered in thick ice. It's the heart of winter, but the lady in red is not in hibernation; she is walking in winter's wisdom. She knows there is no need to rush forward. She knows she can't hurry spring's thaw. She knows the only way out is through, and she walks in equanimity.

She is a woman who understands the emotions of life and the soul cycle's mysterious ways. She knows all souls need time to retreat and go underground, so they can rebreathe themselves new in time.

Time passes and winter slowly begins to cede way to spring. She continues to walk.

She strolls, in her ruby red robes, knowing exactly what she is doing. She does not fear the unknown. She is not pulled in by what others think or subject to altering her course based on where others are going. Her decisions come from her own keen insight and accord.

She feels things begin to shift as August fades into September fades into October, and the moon cycles from crescent to new to half to full.

New visions come in, and with intent and clarity, she begins to check on the seeds she's been planting. Rose seeds planted in winter, though she doesn't know what color or scope they'll take when they bloom.

She senses they're getting close to the ready, yet the soil is still frozen, and they need more time before the ice thaws, and they'll be ready to break through to the light.

She continues to wait in patience. While the world spins. The voices chatter. Others try and keep up with one another. An old

233

part of her, an ancient voice of fear, remembers a time when she was tempted to listen to the voices and do the same.

She knows now that way of being no longer serves her, and in this winter of her life, she's liberated herself from old ways and old fears. She walks in her truth, in harmony with the voice and the task beating inside.

Around the Aries full moon, winter becomes spring in her inner domain. The icy land gives way to mahogany soil, still covered with sheets of brandied ice. And so, she waits, and tends, in patience watching the ice slowly thaw, sensing movement under the surface, waiting to see what will rise.

Three days after the New Moon in Scorpio, on the day before All Hallows' Eve, a lion meets her there. An animal guide of courage and fortitude, the symbol of Archangel Ariel, the representation of Strength in the tarot. She is guided by the lion to an area where the ice is most thin. Soon it will be full spring and what's waiting underneath will emerge into form.

The ice is bell clear — it won't be long now — and she can see what's underneath. She sees deep roots, as far as the eye can see. Roots that have intertwined and interlaced from the rose seeds planted in this space.

Roots that she realizes are not growing a plant or a bush, but a rose forest, so resolute, it will withstand the test of time.

She waits, in wisdom, understanding, and preparation. It matters not, what's going on around her. She knows in her heart she is whole and complete.

She knows. She trusts. She follows her own flow. She waits in the ready and believes.

Somewhere in the distance, a new voice is slowly arising into her consciousness. It won't be long now. As she reaches towards them, the words close enough to brush, and she can finally feel the message that's been emerging from her soul's light:

Rise. It is time. Begin your rise.

121

No! Is a Holy Word

"Yes," binds my ankles and hands, pulling me under.
I've been drowning in a sea of voluntary consent for years,
with nobody to blame but me. What I wish to be,
would like to be, want to learn to be after 40 years
of "yeses," is the kind of woman who simply says "No."
— EMPATH'S LAMENT, *TRANSFORMATIONS OF THE SUN*

*B*oundaries were incredibly hard for me when I was younger. As an empath, I intuitively and reflexively felt the needs and expectations of others, which made it difficult to say *no* and feel and honor my own need and expectation of self in the matter.

This changed in Kauai. It was a change that happened in small degrees and slight gradations, until this past fall, I realized I'd changed entirely and was walking around a new creature.

There were a few who didn't necessarily like it when I stopped being what they expected of me or needed me to be. But I began to find that walking around without the energetic weight of other's expectations and baggage was so liberating, I didn't want to ever go back to the way things were before.

I've learned now that being unclear is unkind, and it took moving here to fully identify:

1. My own voice and needs.

2. I have a right to express my voice and needs.

3. We are here to embrace and embody our self, so it is vital we express our voice and needs. When we do so, we can become and live a fuller expression of our soul's truth.

These days *no* is easy. It's been game-changing and freeing to realize that hurting myself to meet somebody else's expectation of me is not sustainable. When you have a giant open heart, you want to give. But I've realized there is a difference between giving on our own terms versus another's.

I've learned it is the difference between inviting somebody to come into my inner well and freely sharing a cup of my water with them compared to having somebody come along and take a cup without my permission, because I have water and they feel entitled to my water.

People are not entitled to our light. Our time. Our energy. Our feedback. Our support. Or any part of ourselves. We give those things out of freedom and love, and when we realize we are not giving of ourselves out of freedom and love then it's time to step back and evaluate our boundaries.

No is a holy, holy word and it is meant to be intelligently used in the service of love towards others and ourselves, so we can keep freeing ourselves to embody our highest expression of soul.

I used to never know how to hold my own channel of self. I would be around others, open myself up as an empath, and shapeshift to meet them where they were at, so they felt fully seen and heard. I never stopped to consider if this was fair, equitable, or perhaps even harmful for me.

These days I've learned to fully see and hear me. I still care about others, but I also know how to hold my own frequency without taking on theirs, and I've learned it's not my job to do so.

The more I hold my own channel of self, the more I become more me. I have to admit, after a lifetime of being what I thought others needed me to be, it feels pretty f'ing fantastic.

122

Ashram of Change

*A*s November comes around, I feel like I'm emerging. Coming out of a deep cave, an ashram of change, that I've been in for the past couple years.

I didn't know I was in my metaphorical ashram, but after the passage of this last year, I can sense and feel the shedding and exiting occurring. As if I've been on a long voyage, a mystic journey, into the mists of myself, where I've collected many new experiences, wisdoms, and gifts.

Like all hero journeys and spiritual quests, it was a deeply vulnerable, testing, and trying space. I needed to completely lose myself, lose who I'd been in Alaska, to gain deeper entry into myself and metamorphosis into who I was meant to become.

A lot of inner work has happened in my ashram: I grieved and healed over Brent. I came to understand my psychic gifts and own them. I learned to speak with the angels. I healed the wound inflicted by being an empath who sponged in and was saturated with too much energy from others back in my Alaska life.

I healed my wound with being a healer and came to recognize healing in new forms. I learned to say *no*. Root out self-doubt and change. I learned, when my life didn't have much monetary value, of my own value: My heart is my greatest wealth. I can hold myself in the steadfast knowledge of the Queen of Swords I am, regardless of what's reflected in my bank account.

I learned unholy grace under extreme pressure. I learned we're never too spiritual to be gritty human. I learned to live by spiritual principles. By trust, intention, prayer and intuition.

Most importantly, I learned to reseed, rewild, and replant my heart into a deeper space. I traveled all this way thinking that what I most needed was outside of me, yet my life experiences on Kauai simply served as exfoliants, which helped scrub and sieve off layers of my old self. The puzzle piece I was missing wasn't outside of me after all, but the internal truths and self-knowledge I unearthed during my search for self.

These days I'm finding I have new legs underneath me. I feel bigger. More expansive. More me. I don't know how to explain it any better than that, except maybe to say: Sometimes we unwittingly create cages inside of ourselves and we don't even realize we're trapped. The irony is that we don't have to stay stuck waiting for somebody to come along and let us out.

We just have to choose to be freed.

123

LEAP

*T*here will come a time when you're going to be asked to leap. It's going to feel so scary your insides will jelly into liquid-lava pools and your heart will drum into fiery-flight frenzy, and your mind will freeze in suspended disbelief because what you're feeling called towards feels so indelibly BIG —

And you're going to do it anyway.

You're going to do it, because some core part of you knows it's the right thing for you to do.

You're going to do it, because the voice of your soul will hold you to it, insisting this brave, big leap will be the genesis for a braver, bigger you.

You're going to do it, because despite your heart's thumpings and pumpings it has been yearning for this moment, this rich opportunity, and waiting for its chance to break through and break out.

You're going to do it, because you've learned how to show up for you. And you've learned, through showing up for you, that spirit will always meet you in that space and help grow something beautiful and revolutionary.

Mostly you're going to do it, because it's who you are, and you never back down from who you are.

But just in case you're reading this, and you need a nudge in the right direction, just in case you've been asking for a sign or confirmation or message from the universe, here it is:

I believe in you. You are brave and you can do it.

Now please go take your leap.

124

Spotlight

"It is safe to be seen and be KNOWN
as my highest expressions of self."

S ince August, I've been working with the mantra, "It is safe
to be seen and become my highest expression of self." Then
last week the words spontaneously changed into, "be seen and be
known," and then I found myself doing something that shocked
even me.

I don't know what got into me. Actually, that's not true, I do. It
was a vision and a dream that came to me last week along with those
words. So big and scary it feels like life was suspended during that
time, as I was invited to take in, ingest, and integrate this vision.

Could I really? Am I ready? Will anybody want to come?

It started with talking to a fellow heart-centered, ambitious
businesswoman who mentioned she still travels back to her home
state to do workshops and work with coaching clients.

This left me thoughtfully reflecting on Alaska. How I still
have so many people there. How I have all sorts of connections.
What might it look like to go back there for an event?

As I followed the threads of that idea, they began to form a
greater vision:

An auditorium. A stage. A spotlight.

When I first started thinking about going back to Alaska, I
was thinking of a woman's circle. Something safe and easy. Fun
and low pressure, where I know I'll be well received. I'm most at
home when I'm leading women's circles. I know how to do that.

Then the idea of the auditorium started pulling at me. I can
feel myself on a stage, picture the audience before me. I can see
myself giving an inspirational talk. It feels like the most organic
thing in the world in my heart's eye.

More importantly, the restless part of myself — the part who
felt trapped behind a gate last year, who often paces up and down

my insides because she knows there is something more she's supposed to be doing — stops pacing at this vision, and say, *Yes.*

It takes about a week of my stomach bottoming out and doing backflips mixed with trampoline jumps. It takes about a week of my palms sweating and my hands shaking every time I think of it. It takes about a week of grounding trail runs to try and control my mind buzz and mental flight.

It takes about a week, and then I contact the library and rent a theater.

I can feel the talk wanting to write itself, before I've even sat down to write it. *Transform Your Heart. Transform Your World: 8 keys to unlocking your true self.*

I can feel that all the difficult experiences I've been through since I've moved here are ingredients I can convert into this talk. They are my keys:

1. Our hardships holds alchemical power that has the potential to transform us.

2. The intelligence of the heart will guide us through hardship when we listen to its wisdom.

3. We have to say *yes* to our dreams and give ourselves permission.

4. Disillusionment is a potential doorway to deeper authenticity.

5. If we are truly seeking personal growth, then how we think it's going to happen will be different than how it actually happens.

6. The energy of love is wild and wise, and we can trust it.

7. If we want to become a higher expression of self, we have to heal our wound with self-trust.

8. When we choose love, we innately align with our true selves.

I can feel everything I need to do this is already inside of me.

When I finally relax into it, I realize that I don't need to be fearful or nervous or "who am I to do this?" because that's old, broken, retired stuff.

That's an old story of self-doubt and limiting beliefs and playing small. I can feel I'm no longer small. I'm Big. I'm Ready. I'm not afraid.

These days I'm writing a new story, and so far, I like what's on the pages very much.

125

RED YARN

It is a bold
new world,
if you let it —

Filled with
the possibility
of You.
Of Now.

Life may not
have looked
the way you
expected;
unraveling its
shape into a pile
of red yarn at
your feet,
once knit
with the hopes
of your heart.

But in its
undoing you've
been given
a gift: *(I'll tell
you a secret —)*

There is grace
in the mess
and new paths
to find among
those scarlet
ropes, if you
learn to follow

the direction
love takes you.

None of it
was a mistake,
and none of it
in vain: *You
are exactly
where you are
supposed to be —
Remember that.*

Standing there,
cardinal string
bravely clasped
in hand, ready
to receive Life's
beginning and
let it lead you
where it will.

(I'll tell you
another secret —)
*You cannot
possibly lose
your way:*

All roads lead
back to love.

126

Butterfly Effect

definition: a property of chaotic systems
(such as the atmosphere) by which small changes
in initial conditions can lead to large-scale and
unpredictable variation in the future state of the system
— MERRIAM WEBSTER DICTIONARY

*I*t starts with a *yes.*
The *yes* is usually said in a quiet space, on a lonely night, when you're listening deeply, and you decide you can no longer ignore the insistence of the voice within.

You whisper your *yes* out into the stars, wondering if anyone is listening. Even though you may be terrified of what your *yes* may mean, you feel your heart nod in resounding accord.

You begin to allow yourself the possibility of more. The possibility of your possibility, and what might happen if you let go and surrender into unfolding.

Slowly, perhaps quickly, things begin to shift. You begin to see space and movement where you perceived none before.

The more space you find, the more you allow yourself to unfold and let go as you feel and grow into your possibility.

You might even have to shake up your life to do so. Releasing, recanting, resetting, relocating — your heart thrums stronger with each brave shake.

Except the path doesn't look as you expect. You thought you were heading right, then the universe gives you a left. You thought you were heading up, when instead you wind up falling down. You thought you were walking forward, then you find yourself, seemingly, stepping back.

You keep on saying *yes.* Moving slowly, moving sideways, still moving towards.

What you may or may not realize is that when you gave your *yes* in that quiet space long ago, your yes became an answer of YES to spirit. YES, to your soul. YES, to your higher self.

YES, you will open yourself to the change process that will allow you to become your most authentic expression of self.

Your YES sets into motion a cycle of events like the butterfly effect. Each one cascading into the next, impacting, tipping, and affecting the entire ecosystem that is you, offering you the exact ingredients you need to become a more authentic expression.

The ingredients aren't what you expected. Some of them are tricksters — things disguised as something seemingly bad so they trick you into new learning and growth.

But as you begin to look back, over the rocky road you've walked, crawled and swam to make it this far — you begin to see when you mix the ingredients together, you've been given exactly what you needed to experience, expand and know.

Your YES created the butterfly effect, where your soul and the universe conspired to bring into material form whatever you needed for highest growth.

As you keep stepping forward on the path you're creating with each new step of courage, you realize how far you've truly traveled from what you knew then to what you now know. You realize you are *doing it*. You are staking claim to your life, your heart your dreams — embodying a fuller expression of soul.

127

Passages

I 'm not sure if it was Frodo barking at the pigs that woke me or a dream about this book. I just know it's 3:25 a.m. as I write these words, and I simultaneously awoke to a pink pig noisily rolling in the dirt ten feet from our screen window, an irate Frodo noisily barking at him, and a fading dream whose last words I remember: *"All things break through towards the light in their own time."*

I wrote those words last month, and as I have found with my writing, which often prophetically prepares me for a new truth about to emerge, I received a message yesterday from my ancestors about breaking out and stepping into the light at this time.

It was All Soul's Day, also our 4th wedding anniversary, and the day was magical in its own way. I could feel the energy shift around me in the morning, feathers and bells at my back, a sense of presence, the tingling that happens when I know I'm to pick up a pen or my laptop — whatever's closest — and transcribe to the best of my ability whatever is about to come through.

Later that day we went for a run in the mahogany forest in Kilauea. Since we met in a marathon, running is always part of our anniversary celebration.

The day is cloudy, the trees are emerald green and high, horses free roam parts of the trail, a clear pond with lily pads and pink flowers captures my attention, and I stop while Frodo drinks. I smile at the pink flowers, thinking about the metaphor of how lotuses need to root into the mud before prospering and blooming into the light.

It is a strange thing to write a trilogy whose passages you've lived one page at a time. My memory timeline says this last week in October, back in 2016, is when I first turned the original draft of *Lamentations of The Sea* into my publisher.

I have memories of a final Alaskan fall; a heightened appreciation for the golden leaves and hazel ground, soon to be covered with snow and frost. I wrote the final passage for the book on the morning of my mom's birthday. The words woke me before dawn, I crawled out and typed them, knowing I'd just composed the end. That night we took her out for Mexican and bought her roses.

I edited, rearranged, and allowed the story to spool itself through me and weave words into blank sections, so it pulled together into a greater composition. 111 passages of grief, love, loss and letting go.

When I wrote *Transformations of the Sun*, the process surprised me, as the story let me know the sequel I envisioned was actually a trilogy. I was not ready for the final book, but I was meant to write the bridge that travels the story from where it began to where it would end.

The story told itself through me in the spring of 2018, as I collected, revised, revisited, and wrote through misty jungle days, high blue skies, and shifting clouds, which speak to the constant flow of weather change on the island. 122 passages on finding new life after loss.

I moved into the summer of 2018 knowing I would be writing one final book whose pages I'd yet to live. I vividly remember wondering what would fill those passages and how I'd know when the book was done?

As I said in the introduction of this book, an introduction that flew into my mind today as we passed through red dirt trails, rolling green hills and columns of mahogany trees —

I have a unique intuitive process, and in many ways, I believe the story was writing me before I wrote the story. That is how the soul unfolds: it writes us and sings us and moves us into being when we say yes to its call.

The words of this book are pieces of my soul's journey, and now I know I needn't have wondered or worried how I'd know how and when to end. My soul was always going to intuitively sense the right time and know when the larger cycle, whose story is contained in all three books, was ending, so a new one could begin.

The passage of time is a strange thing indeed. We live stories within stories, whose words overlap each other, each one weaving into the other, all of them weaving into the greater story of our soul's unfolding.

We mark our stories by anniversaries and remembering, by honoring and reflecting. We write new stories with the memories we create and weave those into the greater lore of our lives. Every closing an opening, every opening a closing, in endless composition and symphony.

Finishing this book is not THE ending, but it is an ending and it's time. It's unfolded into a sense of whole and completion, and I know I have new things to write and everything is about to change again — I can sense it — even if I don't know exactly what that looks like.

You're ready now. You've fully transplanted and developed deep roots. The kind that can't be shaken or tangled with another's who may lead you astray. You will not lose yourself or sight of yourself on another's path.

Those words are but part of the message that came through from the ancestors this morning, and I feel them. I feel my readiness, I thought I was so ready to become more visible and take the stage at the start of 2019. Now I see the necessity of growth that happened instead. I called 2019 the year of prosperity and spotlight, and I learned my true prosperity is the wealth of love within my heart, and the true spotlight is my ability to hold space for the light and make choices in my life that invite in more light.

We're proud of you. We see you. We see how far you've come. How you've learned to choose love and hold light in innovative ways. We know receiving has been hard for you but stay open and look for our blessing over the coming days and weeks. It's coming. It's coming. Your heart will know when you receive it like sunlight and rain. It will nourish you and assist you. We love you.

I don't know, as I write this, if this particular passage will make it into the final manuscript when I submit my 133. The words above are holy and sacred, gifted to me because I have done the deep work of inner soul. Yet, if I should choose to leave these sacred words in this text, I would offer to anyone who reads them: *You too are seen and blessed by your ancestral lines and the angels who have been guiding your family for generations.*

If you've traveled the passages of these books with me, then you know I didn't start out here. I arrived here because I'm allowing myself to become a higher expression, saying *yes* every time my soul calls me to grow.

These words are simply a possibility of the astounding and magical things that can happen when we return to our heart, again and again, over and over, and let love be our guide, our teacher and our connector to the divine.

You too are loved, you too can access spirit's voice in greater ways that speaks to you, in ways you resonate and hear. You just have to believe, go into your heart-still space, begin the dialogue then watch as your own story unspools.

We ended our anniversary evening with the movie classic — *Lord of the Rings.* The words of that lore have woven themselves into our lives in many forms.

Into the names of our animal companions. Into the memories I shared with Brent; we spoke Tolkien well, him and I. Into the memories I have with my husband from early on when all we wanted to do was learn each other's story and our mutual love of that trilogy entered the conversation.

That's the beautiful thing about stories, we keep reworking them, retelling them, taking elements of them and spinning them into our personal myth, tale and legend. They change as we learn new truths and begin to see our stories from a different lens.

I thought about this story as I ran today. My story. The story of us that is Eric and I. We talked as we ran, though occasionally he would find I'd fallen behind, running slower while speaking into my phone's audio recorder to record ideas coming in for this book.

I thought about the 133 passage that complete these pages and how I only have a few passages left, just a few blank pages, without designated words or content.

The chocolate forest, mossy trees, sage bark and sloping views passed as we created a new memory to add to our anniversary lore. Near the end of our run as the dedication, introduction, and a few other ideas were flying in so fast I had slowed to a jog, so I could record my thoughts and not lose my inspiration, I had a thought for one of the final passages I'd yet to write:

Why don't you write a reflection on the strangely, beautiful intuitive process of writing this book, a breathing and living story that continues to unfold and spool you into bigger being?

You can call it Passages.

128

A Letter to My Younger Self

Dear Younger Self,

I love you. You need to know that. You also need to know your heart is mighty enough to love yourself forward and free yourself.

There are a few things I'd like to take the time to tell you. These are rare gems I've polished and gleamed, because I am you, and I did the inner work to carefully craft these hard-earned wisdoms. (YOU are doing the work, right now, to carefully craft these hard-earned wisdoms. I'm so proud of you for that.)

The first thing I want to share is your grief will always be an opportunity for self-love. Always. It will always afford you the invitation to return to yourself, honor your feelings, and bear reverent witness to the journey of your life.

You never need be afraid of your grief, because it is a doorway in disguise, which will only lead you deeper into love.

Next, you need to know spiritual awakenings can happen more than once.

I know this is a hard one. This will often feel unfair and you will wonder why others might seem to have more ease than you, and yet you are not others. Your soul path is unique, and I promise you it is leading to something grander than what you're currently imagining.

Something else I feel you need to know is: *If you're giving to others out of obligation, it creates an energetic debt, because on some level you feel you owe someone that obligation.*

It is no longer an even exchange and it's not fair for you and your heart. A time is coming when you're going to need to reset and restructure your boundaries. In fact, you have already done this to some degree, but there will be more.

You're going to be ready and able to speak your truth with clarity and release yourself from any relationship whose expectations of you do not serve you. Because, my dear girl, you are here to embody the possibility of you and not somebody's idea of you. It is okay to break up with somebody's idea of you, so you become freer to be and love as yourself.

I also want to share a few things about gratitude, because cultivating gratitude and appreciation is a foundational piece for a happy heart. I need you to know if you ever lose your sense of gratitude, you will have what you need to bring yourself back to a space of thanks.

The universe thrives when appreciation is offered from the heart, and your soul will become a little more alive, every time you say thanks. Gratitude nourishes and blooms us like sunshine, water, and soil do for a plant.

Speaking of the heart, there will be times where you feel your heart contract and break. This is okay, it will always learn how to heal itself.

At times we need to protect and close our hearts while in transformation. You haven't done anything wrong — sometimes the heart, just like a crab, goes inward inside its shell and sets a boundary to buffer against the pain.

Trust your heart though, my dear girl, because you will always find a way to reopen.

Remember a big expansion will always come after a contraction. It is the law of the natural world, and it's helpful for you to remember how a heavy heart feels so you can experience heightened light and joy every time your heart reopens.

Another thing (make sure to write this one down, because you will live its truth in powerful ways):

Investing in maintaining a smaller version of yourself will only prolong your rise. And dear girl, I am here to promise you — you ARE going to rise.

This next thing I want to share is crucial: There is going to be a time, which will feel like one of your darkest hours. You will feel crushed and flattened by the circumstances in your life. You may feel abandoned by the universe and alone on your path of soul.

These feelings are okay. Stay with them and trace them deeper into the cave of your heart. They are illusions rooted in old fears, which tell you you've been forgotten by the Divine. They are not true, and you will figure that out.

In that darkest moment, you will see that your soul has been supporting you all along. Provoking, invoking, and evoking the exact events you will need to become your highest expression of self.

The hardships and challenges and griefs you've experienced are not there to ensnare you, but to help you free yourself to fully return to the truth of who you are, you beautiful, HUGE, diamond soul.

Something else is going to happen in this space, this time of need, where your heart is twisted and crushed: You will begin to hear the archangels speak with such clarity you will wonder how you ever thought you were alone.

They will be your friends and guide you. They will bring you messages of light for yourself and others. You will feel them at your back and before you. This will break your heart, in the best of ways, because it will continue to open you up to the beauty, light, and support coming through.

Mostly, I want you to know that you are going to be okay. That it was always all unfolding according to the pattern of your soul.

I love you so much and I can't wait for you to experience what's coming for you.

You thought you were building a castle when you were building a city.

You thought you were blooming as the lone rose when you were about to burst forth as an ever-giving garden.

You thought you were a plant when you were a sacred, magical, mighty orchard.

You thought you were a fish when you were the magnificence of the ancient wise whales.

Don't mistake yourself again.

Now go forward and be blessed in love.

129

The Things Michael Said

*K*eep calling on us. Keep calling on us in all things and we will bless you and keep you and give you strength.

Uriel will teach you how to shine so you are not afraid of your light.

Raphael will teach you how to be a healer for yourself and others, helping you realize every time you heal your own wounds you shall help others do the same. Do not be afraid to be the wounded healer: you may be punctured many times, yet you will always return to the light.

Ariel is your lineage. She will keep you connected to the earth, walk close to the natural world and better understand the medicine of the flowers, animals, and plants. Call on her whenever you are feeling ungrounded, and she will lift you up and deposit you on your feet in full, so you feel steadied and loved.

Chamuel is an anchor in the storm. He helps anchor you so you can be a comfort to others and help embody and teach his light.

Gabriel will light your voice up with passion. Call on her anytime you need to speak or write your truth. And don't forget about Jophiel, for the two work close together in tandem — like a duo of muses and artists who help you find confidence in the voice of your craft.

And I, Michael will keep and protect you. Watch over you and shepherd you towards the light. You need not fear losing the light — YOUR LIGHT is your birthright, and I am the sacred keeper of the light.

It is I Michael — Keeper of the Light, telling you these things. Be at peace child. You have nothing to fear from my light. Focus on the light when things feel dark, call on me and be at peace and focus on the light.

130

FULL CIRCLE

I know now that I never felt fully seen in my Alaska life, because I couldn't see myself through the old ruts, projections, and prior versions of self, which blocked a clear view.

I see myself now, and while the beginning of my life on Kauai hasn't looked the way I thought it would, I sometimes think I may look back and see these tangled, ragged, disheveled, changeful years as the most awful and beautiful of my life. I know more change will come, yet I don't think anything will ever be quite so radically unique as making a break at midlife to start over and reinvent myself.

I see now I am the woman who put everything on the line to honor what is in my heart, and I am the woman who will always find a way to transform adversity into wisdom. Those experiences and self-knowledge are something nobody can ever take from me.

I'm moving into the next cycle of my life with openness, freedom and clarity, curious as to how this next phase will unfold.

There is a question I began to utter as November slowly gave way to December. My question arose after a message from spirit came in that gifted me these words:

"Things are surfacing and rising up from the deep. Change is on the horizon, financial change, emotional change, change in your circumstances. Your challenges will soon be lessened and at an end. Change in other areas of your life as well. Use this time to prepare yourself for the change.

Nourish your body. Water it like plant. Rest your mind and rest your body. Listen to your heart, it will tell you when it's close. Things are close. Things are nearing. There are great plans for you dear one. Plans you will be ready for.

Use this time for clarity. Keep this time with wisdom like a clock-maker who carefully tightens and tinkers with the clogs and screws. Work on your craft. Keep your heart open. And be not afraid."

I begin to ask my question on a daily basis, realizing my question composes my reason for being.

One day I realize the image I once had of the woman in red, who walked through the winter and was guided into seeing the roots growing beneath spring's ice, has shifted.

I no longer see spring's roots, but summer's orchard. A whole grove of trees filled with treasures and gems. White peaches, pink roses, rubies and diamonds grow from their branches: they are the hard-earned wisdoms that come from dedication and commitment to inner work to transmute dark soul lessons into offerings of beauty and light.

The woman in red is sitting beneath a tree, reading a book and waiting. In preparation and knowing, she is holding the space. Nobody is there yet, but she feels they are coming, though she cannot see them.

She is right. If you could see from the perspective of the sky and look down, you would see word is spreading and people are slowly journeying towards the orchard.

As November grows into December that image only becomes stronger and more cemented, my sense of nearing movement becoming stronger.

2020 feels like a new story, and I take spirit's guidance to heart and spend the remaining months of 2019 working on this book, synthesizing my experiences, writing my Alaska talk, caring for my myself, allowing all that has happened on this island to integrate into me, and continuing to ask my question.

Each morning I go to my heart-still space and enter into my meditation time. My time to receive, be aware, tend to my heart, and dialogue with spirit.

Each morning, I settle into my pillows with a glass of water and a cup of tea. Light a few candles. Burn some incense or cleansing cedar. Place my hand on my heart, close my eyes, and breathe deep as I enter this holy space and ask:

"I am listening. I am here. How can I serve the highest cause of Love?"

131

These Last Words on Grief

I love you.
I miss you.
I always will.

Losing you
changed me —
it always will.

I'm okay
with that,
even as I wish,
it wasn't real —

Because
missing you
keeps changing me,
and so, it shall.

And losing you
keeps rearranging me —
even still.

Now carrying you
is part of me,
within the deepest
heart of me,
I'll miss you 'til
my soul is free
and so, until —

I always will.

132

LEGACY OF LOVE

*A*s I move forward in my life, without the material existence of my brother, what saddens and grieves me the most is the thought of saying goodbye to my parents without him.

We did it all backward in our family. Brent left first, when he should have left after Mom and Dad. There may always be a part of myself who feels it just wasn't meant to be this way. Even as another part accepts this is the way it is: sometimes life unfolds in contrary ways.

I never expected I'd become an only child at midlife, and I often wonder how I'll feel as five years, then ten years, and fifteen years pass without him here? What happens if I reach 77 and will officially have lived half my life without him?

Despite the fact I've been gifted with the immense knowledge of his ongoing presence, such thoughts still curl and tug the mind of a grieving sister, and I think a lot about what my life will look like as I move forward.

Who I will be, who I'll become, what will my contribution be?

Brent never had children and I don't have children, and so the Kapansky name will end with me. This is why Kapansky is still a part of my formal name:

I desire to leave something of heritage that will continue to give to others and allow our family to live on in spirit and nomenclature long after I've left.

❋

I realized, back in the fall — during an in-between space that occurred after the worst of last summer's breaking and before my rebirth of new vision — that I was being called into greater leadership as part of my empowered service in this life.

I don't know how that will look, and I don't need to. I've embraced the idea it's better to surrender the how to the universe and leave it up to the light to decide.

I do know I have been given grave and great experiences these past few years to help me understand the nature of transformation and change and how the fires in our life hold the potential to burn away all that isn't real, so we can become our true selves.

I know my gifts of writing, speaking, intuition, psychology and creativity will be alchemized into helping me step into my role as a leader and share my spiritual teachings with others on greater platforms. This is the vision I see most clearly in my heart and the only logical and intuitive explanation I can think of for why I was ushered through such rapid-fire change in my brief 31 months on the island.

Sometimes the easiest route up to the mountain top is not the quickest, and we take the steepest, bloodiest path to the top to reach a new level in the most efficient manner possible.

I feel this in my personal journey, and I feel that despite my sometimes bloodied knees and winded breath, I traveled a long distance in a short amount of time so I could reach a new level where I was ready to surrender the life I thought was mine, and say *yes* to the life my soul truly has planned for me.

I understand now I did it backwards when I came here.

I created a vision from the inside out, without really knowing what I was trying to build or having a complete direction for my service.

I just followed my inclinations and intuitions and heart-musings and haphazard-ed my platform together based on what felt good to my heart, not what I believed would sell.

I am who I am, because I'm a contrarian who refuses to fit a mold and be anyone other than what my heart directs. Sometimes our hearts unfold in contrary ways, yet one thing I've learned in deeper forms since losing Brent is that I will always answer *yes* when the truth of my heart gives me a directive.

Even when I know *yes* won't look the way I think it will.

Even when I know *yes* will sometimes domino our lives apart to help us rebuild a structure that better supports us.

Even when I know saying *yes* to this path means releasing my hold on all aspects of my life, so I can live in a space of deep trust and surrender.

I didn't come here to leave any stone unturned or experience unlived or leap untaken. I came here to become my highest expression of self, and so I will keep saying *yes*, no matter.

❀

I believe I was always going to arrive at the destination of wanting to serve Love in bright and powerful ways. I've been following the wilderness of my heart for over a decade now, and I believe its rugged terrain and vast seas would have rivered me to a life of deep purpose and soulful meaning.

Yet it is impossible to not acknowledge when I lost Brent, grief's alchemy created a new passageway, which led me into a more multidimensional existence of courage, magic, grace and love.

Losing Brent and choosing to see, feel and know my grief as a holy rite of passage forced me to take the steep route up the mountain, and arrive at this destination more quickly than I would have otherwise.

I don't know that I would have found the courage to leave my Alaska life when I did, to say *yes* to myself in these terrifying, exhilarating ways, if not for Brent.

Every day as I move forward in my life, I am aware that much of my journey has played out because my heart dared to ask the question, *"How can my grief help me love and live braver, better and bigger and who might I become if I did so?"*

I am not who I am solely because of Brent, yet because of Brent I've become who I am.

These are the bittersweet musings that riddle me when I allow myself to delve into my grief and taproot its deepest sorrows. These are the thoughts that drive my desire and motivate my passion.

❀

Grief and love are the major themes of this trilogy, but I think, equally, so is trust.

I have been asked to unconditionally trust my process, my life, myself, my spiritual connection, and my dreams and intentions in the face of struggle, hardship, and a lack of evidence the visions of my heart will manifest into fruition.

Our culture operates under the mistaken assumption that we have to see it to believe it, and yet I have learned we have to believe it to see it. It's backward thinking to some, and yet truth often unfolds in contrary ways.

You see, truth is alive in love, and love is a sacred, rebellious force, which will go to any lengths to help bring us closer to the truth of who we are.

I believe a day will come where I look back on this time in my life and see it as an obfuscated grace. A dark grace that covered me and ultimately helped me be more me. I believe I will better comprehend I was part of a bigger plan, and my soul needed time, space, and protection to liberate its depth and fullness.

I trust my soul now. I trust my work. I trust my process. I trust spirit. I trust life.

I even trust my grief.

I'm not afraid of my grief anymore, for it has only brought me into deeper love, deeper light, and a deeper understanding of change, transformation and the sacred cycles of life.

❀

A lone songbird chirps outside in the murky jungle green as I write these final thoughts. I realize I started this essay with a destination in mind and find the words have spiraled me somewhere else entirely.

Sometimes stories unfold in contrary ways, and we travel backwards and sideways to circle us around to the beginning.

Which brings me back to where this next to last passage began:

As I move forward in my life, without the material existence of my brother still here, what haunts me the most is the thought of saying goodbye to my parents without him.

We did it backward in our family, he left first, when he should have left after Mom and Dad... Sometimes life unfolds in contrary ways.

I never expected I'd become an only child at midlife, and I often wonder how I'll feel as five years, then ten years, and fifteen years pass without him here? What happens if I reach 77 and will officially have lived half my life without him?

My parents are in their golden years, and I often wonder how much time each of them will have, even as I choose to release worry and appreciate the time we have been given.

I seek to find joy and savor the memories we create together in our changed family constellation, because someday it will be just me. They will join Brent and begin their journey down the hallway of light, through the house of healing, into the eternal realms of soul.

Someday I know I will cross the bridge of what it feels like to be the last Kapansky standing, and I will say *goodbye* and *see you again* to my parents.

Someday I know I will see Brent again too.

Though none of us truly knows the day or time of our death, I intuitively feel it's highly likely I will make that 77-year-old benchmark. Because I've got work to do and after two and a half years of going through intense, profound transformation in Kauai, I am more assured than ever: I am just getting started.

I have a Legacy of Love to build, and I'm moving forwards in openness and trust as to how that unfolds.

In the meantime, as I pen this last bit of my memoir, there are words that have just appeared in my mind. First written in a poem in *Lamentations*, they are insistently informing me they are the perfect note with which to end:

"There is a place not far from here, where there is grace and no condemnation. Someday I will meet you, and we shall be free.

But not yet, my brother. Not yet."

133

THOR'S HAMMER

*L*ittle Sister listen up! It's time. It's time to set yourself loose on the world. It's coming for you and you're coming for it. Don't be afraid of what's coming your way. You were born for this. You are meant for this. I'm still here guiding you and watching your back.

You need to remember you're strong and mighty, like Thor in *Avengers* when he realizes he doesn't need his hammer. Yes, I was there watching it with you, and the hammer is just a tool. He's the power. These gifts you have, they are your tools. But it is you who brings the light, you who holds the light. You are the power.

I'm so proud of you. I love you. Tell Mom and Dad I love them too.

I'm still me, but different now. It's better up here than anyone can possibly imagine. And I'm so happy. You need to know that. I want you to be happy too.

You did it, Little Sister, you became the rose who learned to bloom in winter. Don't stop believing. You are so close.

If you need me, call me. Call me in your heart, speak to me in your heart. Tell everybody to speak to us in their hearts, their loved ones on the other side. We are listening. We are guiding. We will be there.

We're only a heart call away.

Little Sister, I'm only a heart call away.

Epilogue: The End is the Begin

"What we call the beginning is often the end.
And to make an end is to make a beginning.
The end is where we start from."

— T.S. ELIOT

I have to admit some part of me wanted to end this book with a triumphant moment that somehow equated material success and the actualization of my dreams.

One of my books made it big.

I got offered a huge speaking engagement.

Oprah called.

But I did not name this book "Manifestations of The Earth." I named it "Revelations of The Sky," and so it was. This final book is about my spiritual journey, my inner work and how the more I tunneled deeper into the space of my heart, the more I was able to receive from my intuitive self, my soul and my spiritual connection in profound and meaningful ways.

I suspect if I were to go on to write a fourth book, "Manifestations of The Earth" would be an apt name, because I sense the time is coming that my dreams grow in tangible ways. The last few years cleared a great deal of space in my life to channel love in new ways, and I believe my greater work is just getting started.

But this is a trilogy, not a quartet, and it's time to end this and move on to write new tales and find new truths. The end is just the beginning. We will forever be weaving our stories as we go, each new strand intersecting and connecting our souls in a deeper web of truth.

If I could leave you with one final thought, I would leave you with the idea these books have been a love story. Told in three parts. A collection of what I believe will prove to be the most transformative years of my life, and I wrote it all down so if anybody ever asks me:

How do you find the light and perspectives you have on grief?

I will say: *It began with love.*

If they should ask me: *How did you learn to talk to the angels?*

I will say: *It began with love.*

If I should be gifted to live into my golden years, and I am looking back on the legacy of love I did indeed create, in whatever form spirit directs me, and somebody should ask:

What inspired you to start down this path?

I will say: *It began with love.*

My personal story is a story within the greater story of these books which explore the possibility of what happens when we allow and surrender to love.

Love is intelligent, creative, wise, and unruled. It will always seek to free itself to become a bigger expression. When we nourish the energy of love in our hearts, love can heal, change, shape and reveal us.

Love creates magic, miracles and boldness in our lives. This is the eternal truth our souls seek, and our paths unfold in such a way to try to help us become liberated by love's truth.

And so, the story ends where it began: with love. An ongoing ouroboros of transformation, shedding, releasing, growing and re-birthing every time we choose it. Love is the end and the begin.

Namaste. Blessed be. Amen.

With love,
Dr. BethAnne K.W.

CLOSING CREDITS

A few acknowledgments and inspirations:

In *Ramble on Rose* the lyrics used are from "Ramble on Rose" as written by Robert C. Hunter and Jerome J. Garcia. In *Ship of Fools*, the lyrics used are from "Ship of Fools" as written by Robert Plant. My deep apologies to any hardcore Dead fans who noticed I reference the Dead's version of the song, then used a quote from another song of the same title. I took artistic liberty.

Both *Lion Heart* and *The Contrarian* were originally published in *Things of that Nature: words for the mystic heart* (Golden Dragonfly Press, 2019). *Red Yarn* was originally published in *Heliotrope Nights: starlight for the mind and soul* (Golden Dragonfly Press, 2017). The quote at the end of *Loving Ourselves Whole After Loss* is from the passage *Infinite* in *Lamentations of The Sea* (Golden Dragonfly Press, 2017).

In *Burn*, the quote from the card "Volcano" is from the *Iris Oracle* written and created by Mary Elizabeth Evans. In *The Illusion*, the reference to the card *Discernment* is from Alana Fairchild's *Crystal Mandala Oracle Deck*.

Several movie inspirations have made their way into these pages: The reference to Mr. Miyagi in *New Breeze* is a reference to the character from the movie Karate Kid. All references to Luke Skywalker, Yoda and Obi-Wan scattered throughout are from the *Star Wars* movies. In Thor's Hammer, the movie referenced is the *Avengers: Infinity War*. The last line quoted in Legacy of Love is inspired by the final line in the movie *Gladiator*, "Now we are free. I will see you again, but not yet. Not yet."

A few words of thanks:

I have so much gratitude and warmth to express to the women who reviewed this work in advance for me. In no particular order and with all the love: Catherine Schweig, April M. Lee, Janet Venturini, Tammy Stone Takahashi, Kris Franken, and Dr. Alyse Snyder — THANK YOU! I appreciate the time you took to review this manuscript and all your words of support. I feel so grateful and fortunate to be surrounded by such a beautiful group of women who bring so many talents to this world, professionally and personally. I thank you from my heart.

My deepest gratitude to my friend and colleague Carolyn Riker for reviewing, editing, sound-boarding, daisy-chaining, friending and supporting me through this whole process.

Last, but not at all least — my appreciation and heartfelt thanks to Alice Maldonado for publishing the *Lamentations Trilogy* and welcoming my work and my words into Golden Dragonfly Press. Thank you for being with me for the whole of this trilogy journey and helping the words on these pages become a tangible reality.

About the Author

BethAnne Kapansky Wright, PsyD, is deeply passionate about inspiring authentic change in others. A Spiritual Psychologist, Intuitive Channel, Writer, Speaker and Artist she blends the worlds of psychology and spirit to offer dynamic teaching on healing and transforming our relationship with ourselves.

She is the author of the award-winning grief book, *Lamentations of The Sea* and its sequel *Transformations of The Sun*, as well as several books of poetry and a children's book. Through her writing, in-person talks, and online courses, she uses a variety of creative mediums to inspire others to find their heart magic and step into their divine potential.

Her life underwent profound change when she lost her brother in 2016, which became the catalyst for leaving her longtime home of Alaska and moving to the island of Kauai to live more intuitively, spiritually, and creatively.

Website: www.bethannekw.com

IG: @dr.bethannekw

FB: Dr. BethAnne KW

For intuitive guidance and updates on my books, courses and speaking events, sign up for my monthly letter!

IntuitiveYOU@bethannekw.com

Also by Dr. BethAnne K.W.

Grief & Loss

LAMENTATIONS OF THE SEA: 111 Passages on Grief, Love, Loss, and Letting Go. Winner of the 2017 Silver Nautilus Award for Grief and Loss

TRANSFORMATIONS OF THE SUN: 122 passages on finding new life after loss

Poetry & Prose

THINGS OF THAT NATURE: Words for the Mystic Heart

HELIOTROPE NIGHTS: Starlight for the Mind and Soul

FREEBIRD FRIDAYS: A Love Story

CRANBERRY DUSK: A Journey of Becoming

HIDDEN LIGHTS ANTHOLOGY: A Collection of Truths Not Often Told

Children's Books

TALLULAH TALKS TO NATURE: A Tallulah Adventure